Prayer is the soul's sincere desire,
Uttered or unexpressed,
The motion of a hidden fire
That trembles in the breast.

Prayer is the burden of a sigh,
The falling of a tear,
The upward glancing of an eye
When none but God is near.

Prayer is the simplest form of speech
That infant lips can try;
Prayer the sublimest strains that reach
The majesty on high.

Prayer is the contrite sinner's voice
Returning from his ways,
While angels in their songs rejoice,
And cry: "Behold, he prays!"

Prayer is the Christian's vital breath,
The Christian's native air,
Our watchword at the gate of death;
We enter heaven with prayer.

O thou by whom we come to God,
The Life, the Truth, the Way!
The path of prayer thyself hast trod:
Lord, teach us how to pray!

JAMES MONTGOMERY (1771-1854)

PRAYING JESUS' WAY

A Guide for Beginners
& Veterans

Brian J. Dodd

InterVarsity Press
Downers Grove, Illinois

InterVarsity Press® is the book-publishing division of InterVarsity Christian Fellowship®, a student movement active on campus at hundreds of universities, colleges and schools of nursing in the United States of America, and a member movement of the International Fellowship of Evangelical Students. For information about local and regional activities, write Public Relations Dept., InterVarsity Christian Fellowship, 6400 Schroeder Rd., P.O. Box 7895, Madison, WI 53707-7895.

Cover photograph: Giraudon / Art Resourse, NY. Andrea Mantegna. Christ in the Garden, detail. Musée des Beaux-Arts, Tours, France.

ISBN 0-8308-1993-2

Printed in the United States of America ♾

Library of Congress Cataloging-in-Publication Data

Dodd, Brian J., 1960-
    Praying Jesus' way: a guide for beginners & veterans / Brian J. Dodd.
      p.   cm.
    Includes bibliographical references.
    ISBN 0-8308-1993-2 (alk. paper)
    1. Jesus Christ—Prayers.   2. Prayer—Christianity.   I. Title.
BV229.D63   1997
248.3'2—dc21   96-48376
                                                                        CIP

| 19 | 18 | 17 | 16 | 15 | 14 | 13 | 12 | 11 | 10 | 9 | 8 | 7 | 6 | 5 | 4 | 3 | 2 |
| 12 | 11 | 10 | 09 | 08 | 07 | 06 | 05 | 04 | 03 | 02 | 01 | 00 | 99 | 98 | 97 |

For Julia, Kirstie, Karen and Jeff
With special gratitude for
all I am learning about prayer
from my wife Ingrid and
God's people in Antioch

1

Introduction
Praying Jesus' Way

You probably picked up this book for the same reason that I wrote it. Prayer is very important to me, and yet it is a struggle. I am determined to pray regularly, but I continue to battle with lack of motivation and shortage of time. The problem is not that I undervalue prayer. On the contrary, I firmly believe that prayer is crucial to our relationship with God, providing the foundation of peace and joy that can only come from intimacy with the Creator. I wholeheartedly agree with Martin Luther, who said that prayer is "the real calling of all Christians," and with Origen, the early church father who called prayer "the heart of all piety."[1]

The problem for me—and maybe for you—is that praying remains a struggle. When the subject of prayer comes up, I tend to feel spiritually inadequate, and I have found that many Christians feel guilt and shame about the lack of quality and quantity time they spend communing with God. Perhaps it is precisely because we believe prayer is so important that we often feel so inadequate—even guilty—about how feebly or seldom we pray alone. For many of us, Sunday worship is a reminder that it has been a week since we have spoken with the One who deserves our daily honor and desires our daily attention.

Jesus anticipated our difficulties and gave us some very practical teaching, including concrete examples of how to pray. As we grapple with prayer, we can take encouragement from the fact that the earliest Christians admitted that they struggled too. The great missionary Paul candidly confesses, "We do not know how to pray as we ought" (Rom 8:26). Frankly, this gives me some relief, and I am very grateful that Jesus' first disciples requested, "Lord, teach us to pray" (Lk 11:1). It is in response to their struggle (as well as ours) that Jesus teaches us the way forward in our prayer lives. We can be confident that Jesus will help us learn to pray, since prayer flowed as naturally as sleeping and eating in his life. The pages that follow examine Jesus' prayer life and his teaching about prayer so that we, like his first disciples, can follow in his footsteps.

Why Another Book on Prayer?

Why another book on prayer? The question deserves an answer at the beginning. If we were to read all the books that are available on prayer, we would certainly have no time left to pray! This book focuses on Jesus' example and instruction about prayer, especially the Lord's Prayer. Many books on prayer fall into one of two categories: academic studies that tend to be inaccessible to the average Christian and popular-level discussions that are based more on contemporary experience than on focused study of Jesus' precept and practice.[2] This book centers on Jesus' prayers, and it draws on important scholarly discoveries about Jesus' teaching on prayer in its Jewish context in a way that nonspecialists can appreciate.

Jesus' example of prayer has been good news for me in my

struggle with prayer. He shows that God loves simple prayers with few words. Some pray with great boldness and confidence, as if doubt had no place in the life of prayer. But Jesus prays a yielded "your will be done." Some teach techniques for achieving results by prayer, but Jesus tells a simple story of a woman who kept knocking on the same door and kept making the same request. Clearly, Jesus valued tenacity over technique. This book majors on Jesus' encouraging example and his clear directions for our prayer lives. The Lord's Prayer will serve as our outline for understanding Jesus' prayer life and as the chief guide for our prayers as they are patterned after Jesus' prayers.

Praying the "Our Father"
I first encountered a paternoster at the British university where I studied for a few years. This device is a vertical conveyor belt, sort of a cross between an escalator and an elevator. An alternative to waiting ages for the elevator or climbing hundreds of stairs, the paternoster invites the brave and the hurried to leap aboard and get swept aloft. The challenge is to make it onto your car before it pins you to the ceiling and then to exit gracefully without falling on your face. After three years of practice, I began to feel less uncomfortable and found myself opting for the stairs less and less often.

No one knows for sure, but there is a theory about how this elevator-like terror got its name, a combination of the first two words of the Lord's Prayer in Latin—*Pater Noster* ("Our Father"). Occasionally the paternoster freezes up, usually when it is loaded with students, and it is said that the words of the Lord's Prayer echo in the shaft as students wait to get unstuck.

The legend may or may not be true, but prayer came to my mind more than once as I was being swept up and down. It has occurred to me that the paternoster serves well as a metaphor for the Lord's Prayer. Jesus warns us that this world is full of highs and lows. "In this world you will have tribulations." I have come to see the Lord's Prayer, the *Pater Noster* as some traditions call it, as a gift from Jesus that helps us when we are on the mountain heights of the best days of our lives, when we are in the darkest depths of the worst weeks, and when we are stuck in the mundane middle, sometimes for months and years at a time. The Lord's Prayer is his wise gift to teach us to pray and to keep us praying when we feel like giving up.

This is not to say that our prayer life should be limited to repeating the prayers of others. On the contrary, one of Jesus' most important lessons about prayer points out that it is a personal conversation between trusting child and loving Creator. But praying Jesus' prayer can be a help to us, whether we are just beginning to pray or we have long enjoyed the fruits of regular conversation with the Lord.

Following the master's example word for word can teach beginners timeless truths about prayer, which the Jewish people of God passed on to Jesus and Jesus then passed on to us. Education is the shortcut to experience, and following someone else's example is often the shortcut to education. If you want to learn tennis, it helps immensely to study someone else's play. If you want to learn to pray, it helps to pattern yourself after the master Teacher who said, "Follow me" and "Pray then in this way." The Lord's Prayer is for beginners.

But the Lord's Prayer is for veterans too. We sometimes find ourselves falling into ruts and becoming stuck in habits, unable to lift ourselves out of endless, boring repetition. Many people find this true of their prayer lives. There have been times in my life when prayer has been an easy and natural thing, like breathing and smiling. But I have found, and maybe you have too, that the enthusiasm of unstructured prayer wanes, and I start to leave unprayed many things that I really wanted to speak about with the Lord. In fact, structure and discipline can add to the experience of joy and spontaneity. This is how the Lord's Prayer has benefited me, causing me to remember to lift up in prayer all the things that I truly want to express to the Lord about my life and our world. Just as a veteran tennis player needs to focus on the basics to remain good at the sport, so experienced pray-ers need to refresh themselves on the foundational aspects of prayer, and Jesus coaches us through the Lord's Prayer. Prayer warriors can greatly enhance their praying and can ground it more deeply in biblical truths by meditating on, studying and practicing the prayer that Jesus taught us. Experience proves what Thomas Merton, a great man of prayer, has said, "Saying the *Pater Noster* is like swimming in the heart of the sun."[3]

Some readers may benefit most from this book by reading it straight through, while others may read a chapter, mull it over, and digest it before resuming. I am a start-at-the-beginning-and-plod-through kind of reader. My wife, on the other hand, is more of a buffet reader, sampling from here and there until her plate is full and then returning at a later time. This book was written with both types of readers in mind, and the questions for reflection at the end of each chapter are intended to take us from reading about prayer to a deeper experience of praying.

Questions for Reflection

1. How would you rate your private prayer life, on a scale of one to ten? Why?

2. Have you ever felt guilty or ashamed for not praying? Why?

3. What aspects of Jesus' prayer life are you most eager to explore? Skim the table of contents and the relevant chapters to get an overview.

4. What aspects of prayer need strengthening in your life?

2

How Jesus Prayed

A s I was driving my two daughters to school one day, I realized that we had not yet prayed together that morning. So I announced, "Let's pray together for the coming day." I prayed about their school day, the appointments I had, and their mother's new job—matters that I had often prayed about. When I finished praying, I faced intense spiritual controversy and inquisition.

My daughters were used to praying with their eyes closed and their hands folded. Neither of them had missed the fact that I had prayed while I was driving—*with my eyes open*. They immediately demanded an explanation. They always prayed with their eyes closed and thought we had to pray that way. This was a reasonable assumption, since we and their Sunday school teachers had always urged this as a method of crowd control during times of prayer with young children. My younger daughter stuck by the rules—"we are *supposed* to pray with our eyes closed"—

while my older daughter stuck by me.

The only thing that could settle the Great Car Prayer Controversy was an appeal to Jesus' own example. When I said, "Jesus prayed with his eyes open," they were shocked. "He did?" I went on to explain that he probably prayed with his eyes open and his hands lifted to heaven, like other Jews in his day (Jn 17:1; 1 Tim 2:8). Finally my daughters were satisfied. If it's OK for Jesus, it should be OK for Dad. Fortunately they never pressed me with "Dad, did Jesus pray while he drove?"

I am just like my daughters in that Jesus' example settles a lot of issues for me. I want to be like Jesus, and his pattern of prayer is important for me to follow, regardless of the doubts, fears or questions I may have about how prayer works. Jesus practiced what he preached about prayer. His actions and his instruction combine to show us how important prayer is for our life with God. They work in tandem to give us a very clear model that we can duplicate in our lives. If we have reservations about prayer because of the mechanistic and antispiritual culture in which we live, we find much encouragement from the Master, who believed in prayer and practiced it often. Ponder ten characteristics of Jesus' prayer life.

1. Jesus Believed That Prayer Works

Jesus believed in the effectiveness and the possibility of prayer. Sometimes our motivation to pray is killed when we doubt that our prayers make any difference. If prayer doesn't "work," why pray at all? Of course there is much more to prayer than asking, but asking is a big part of it. Jesus gives us needed encouragement because he believed prayer to be effective, and he said so. For those of us who have wondered if prayer really makes a difference, it is uplifting and encouraging to listen to Jesus' boldness and confidence that God hears and answers prayer:

Whatever you ask for in prayer with faith, you will receive. (Mt 21:22)

Ask, and it will be given you; search, and you will find; knock, and the door will be opened for you. For everyone who asks receives, and everyone who searches finds, and for everyone who knocks, the door will be opened. Is there anyone among you who, if your child asks for bread, will give a stone? Or if the child asks for a fish, will give a snake? If you then, who are evil, know how to give good gifts to your children, how much more will your Father in heaven give good things to those who ask him! (Mt 7:7-11)

When he had entered the house, his disciples asked him privately, "Why could we not cast it out?" He said to them, "This kind can come out only through prayer." (Mk 9:28-29)

So I tell you, whatever you ask for in prayer, believe that you have received it, and it will be yours. (Mk 11:24)

I will do whatever you ask in my name, so that the Father may be glorified in the Son. If in my name you ask me for anything, I will do it. (Jn 14:13-14)

If you abide in me, and my words abide in you, ask for whatever you wish, and it will be done for you. (Jn 15:7)

You did not choose me but I chose you. And I appointed you to go and bear fruit, fruit that will last, so that the Father will give you whatever you ask him in my name. (Jn 15:16)

Very truly, I tell you, if you ask anything of the Father in my name, he will give it to you. Until now you have not asked for anything in my name. Ask and you will receive, so that your joy may be complete. (Jn 16:23-24)

As we can see, Jesus often taught that prayer works. He encourages us to pray because God, like a loving father, is overjoyed to fulfill requests made by his children. This teaching does not address the issue of prayers that go unanswered, but it does encourage us to make our requests known to God. Jesus believed and acted on the confidence that God answers prayer.

2. Jesus' Prayers Did Not Make Him Passive

Jesus' prayers did not make him passive. This is a common misstep in the spiritual life. It is wrong to assume that devotion to God and human responsibility are somehow mutually exclusive. It is like a Christian who watched a neighbor turn a weed-filled lot into a beautiful garden. After the project was well underway and the flowers were in bloom, the two came together. The Christian, taking advantage of the opportunity, exclaimed, "Isn't it wonderful what God can do with a piece of land!" Her neighbor retorted, "You should have seen it when God had it all to himself!"

Jesus did not separate prayer from responsibility nor did he separate faith from action. Jesus prayed and he cared; he believed and he acted; he preached the good news of the kingdom of God and he lived under that same rule. In Matthew, Jesus warns against a faith that does not respond to human needs:

When the Son of Man comes in his glory, and all the angels with him, then he will sit on the throne of his glory. All the nations will be gathered before him, and he will separate people one from another as a shepherd separates the sheep from the goats, and he will put the sheep at his right hand and the goats at the left. Then the king will say to those at his right hand, "Come, you that are blessed by my Father, inherit the kingdom prepared for you from the foundation of the world; for I was hungry and you gave me food, I was thirsty and you gave me something to drink, I was a stranger and you welcomed me, I was naked and you gave me clothing, I was sick and you took care of me, I was in prison and you visited me." Then the righteous will answer him, "Lord, when was it that we saw you hungry and gave you food, or thirsty and gave you something to drink? And when was it that we saw you a stranger and welcomed you, or naked and gave you clothing? And when was it that we saw you sick or in prison and visited you?" And the king will answer them, "Truly I tell you, just as you did it to one of the least of these who are members of my family, you did it to me." Then he will say to those at his left hand, "You that are accursed, depart from me into the eternal fire prepared for the devil and his angels; for I was hungry and you gave me no food, I was thirsty and you gave me nothing to drink, I was a stranger and you did not welcome me, naked and you did not give me clothing, sick and in prison and you did not visit me." Then they also will answer, "Lord, when was it that we saw you hungry or thirsty or a stranger or naked or sick or in prison, and did not take care of you?" Then he will answer them, "Truly I tell you, just as you did not do it to one of the least of these, you did not do it to me." And these will go away into eternal punishment, but the righteous into eternal life. (Mt 25:31-46)

Using the strongest possible terms, Jesus rejects a spirituality that is unconcerned about the tangible needs of people around us. Real needs and practical caring matter to God. Prayer is no excuse for failing to act morally. In the words of the apostle Paul, "If I have all faith, so as to remove mountains, but do not have love, I am nothing" (1 Cor 13:2). Instead, as someone has aptly said, "We should pray as though it all depends on God, but act as though it all depends on us."

Keeping the balance between trusting prayer and responsible stewardship is not easy. Some of us tend to err in the other direction, toward a "pull-yourself-up-by-your-own-bootstraps" theology that devalues trusting prayer. Such a theology emphasizes human actions. Its doctrine can be summed up as "God helps those who help themselves," tipping the balance too far toward human independence from God. It tends toward a theology of works and is actually an antigospel sentiment. After all, we have heard in the gospel that God saves those who *can't* save themselves. "For while we were still weak, at the right time Christ died for the ungodly" (Rom 5:6).

Keeping the balance between trusting prayer and faithful

action is essential. God's graciousness does not eclipse human responsibility. On the contrary, God in grace has gifted us and has made us able to care for ourselves and for one another. Even though we are often crippled by our own personal brokenness and the brokenness of the world around us, nevertheless God does provide help through those who do all they can do, even while praying for God's intervention. In the words of John Wesley, the eighteenth-century Anglican reformer,

> Do all the good you can,
>> by all the means you can,
>>> in all the ways you can,
>>>> in all the places you can,
>>>>> at all the times you can,
>>>>>> to all the people you can,
>>>>>>> as long as ever you can.[1]

Like Jesus, we should pray as though it all depended on God, but act responsibly as though it all depended on us.

We should pause and take a test case about prayer and passivity. Consider those who are passive in an abusive relationship with a spouse. Luke 6:28 applies to them, but it is clearly not all they should do: "Bless those who curse you, pray for those who abuse you." This passage makes prayer a part of the longsuffering love of the Christian life. Jesus calls us to remove ourselves from the law of retaliation and to adopt an attitude toward others that reflects God's stance toward us: "Be kind to one another, tenderhearted, forgiving one another, as God in Christ has forgiven you. Therefore be imitators of God, as beloved children, and live in love, as Christ loved us and gave himself up for us, a fragrant offering and sacrifice to God" (Eph 4:32—5:2).

But for too many women, this attitude leads to their own destruction. The title of a popular book says it all: *Women Who Love Too Much*.[2] Longsuffering love does not mean lying down like a doormat. While women in abusive relationships should pray for those who abuse them, they urgently need to remove themselves from the abusive situation and from the abusive relationship. (Those of us who have never been terrorized by a loved one should not underestimate how difficult it is to extract oneself from the cycle of abuse.) In this case prayer and action cannot be pitted against each other. We must pray for those who abuse us, but we must remove ourselves from their abuse consistent with the three-way love command: (1) loving God with all that we are is accompanied by (2) loving our neighbors (3) *as we love ourselves*. Self-care is an essential part of love for God and neighbor, and it is completely compatible with Jesus' command to abandon the law of retaliation. Jesus' prayers did not make him passive, and neither should ours.

3. Jesus Got Alone to Pray

Jesus' first instruction on how to pray in the Gospel of Matthew is a caution not to practice our piety so that others can see us and be impressed by our spirituality (Mt 6:1). He tells us, "Whenever you pray, go into your room and shut the door and pray to your Father who is in secret; and your Father who sees in secret will reward you" (Mt 6:6). Matthew, Mark and Luke tell us that this was typical of Jesus' life:[3]

> In the morning, while it was still very dark, he got up and went out to a deserted place, and there he prayed. And Simon and his companions hunted for him. (Mk 1:35-36)

> He went up the mountain by himself to pray. When evening came, he was there alone. (Mt 14:23)

> But he would withdraw to deserted places and pray. (Lk 5:16)

> He came out and went, as was his custom, to the Mount of Olives;

and the disciples followed him. When he reached the place, he said
to them, "Pray that you may not come into the time of trial." Then
he withdrew from them about a stone's throw, knelt down, and
prayed. (Lk 22:39-41)

The last passage shows us the interconnection that existed
between Jesus' teaching and example. It was Jesus' "custom" to
go out to the Mount of Olives, as well as other deserted places,
to pray (Mt 14:13; Lk 6:12; 9:18). His disciples "follow him"
literally by going with him, but they also imitate his example as
he gives them further instruction on prayer. After Jesus shows
them what to pray about, he follows his own guidance on solitary
prayer: "Then he withdrew from them about a stone's throw,
knelt down, and prayed" (Lk 22:41).

Why does Jesus model solitary prayer? This practice checks
our motivation. We are all susceptible to spiritual pride, and it
often matters far too much what other people think of us. When
we pray alone, we avoid this pitfall (unless we announce to others
how much we pray when we are by ourselves!). If we pray where
people see us, we are prone to enjoy the attention. This is the
explicit reason Jesus gives (Mt 6:5-6).

There is a second reason why private prayer is important.
Simply stated, it is difficult to have two conversations at the
same time. If we pray when other people are around, we are
likely to engage them (or they us) and thus become distracted
from God. We practice this etiquette in our other relationships. Interrupting an important conversation to pay attention to a trivial matter drastically limits the conversation from
going deeper. This is what happens when we take our eternally
important prayer time and break it up to answer the phone or
handle a matter that could wait until we are done giving full
attention to the Ruler of the universe. Jesus used strategic prayer
retreats to avoid distractions:

> At daybreak he departed and went into a deserted place. And the crowds were looking for him; and when they reached him, they wanted to prevent him from leaving them. (Lk 4:42)

> But now more than ever the word about Jesus spread abroad; many crowds would gather to hear him and to be cured of their diseases. But he would withdraw to deserted places and pray. (Lk 5:15-16)

If you have ever struggled with distraction while you are praying, consider Jesus' "geographical cure" to the problem. It is both practical and wise to find an undistracted time and place to pray, just like good students who have a special place to study. The best students know that if they work at a desk reserved for study, they become conditioned to study every time they sit at that desk. Their concentration improves, and they are more able to focus efficiently on the reading or studying at hand.

So it is with prayer. Praying in bed is a case in point. Bed is a place where we sleep. If we try to pray while we are lying in bed, we are setting ourselves up for a short prayer time! For this reason, kneeling next to the bed in prayer is preferable for those of us who want to grow in our times of prayer. This is the only thing I do next to my bed, so when I kneel to pray every fiber in my body and psyche assists me in praying. This is one posture Jesus used to help him focus in prayer (Lk 22:41).

Mothers of small children face a special challenge. The following "True (Prayer) Confessions," which my wife Ingrid wrote for our church newsletter, will sound familiar to those of us who struggle to find times of solitary prayer amid the demands of parenting:

> It's 8:36 Sunday evening, and I've plopped myself down on the couch. The dishwasher is finally loaded and running, the kids are settled for the night, the mountain of Sunday papers has been gathered and neatly stacked, and in a few minutes I'll move a load of laundry from the washer to the dryer. I feel like I need a weekend to recover from the weekend.

So OK Lord, here I am, ready to talk and let you know what's going on. I really wanted to watch *Masterpiece Theater* tonight, but I've decided that I need to beef up the time I spend speaking with you directly, and—as you know—since I'm not breaking any prayer endurance records at the moment that won't be too difficult to do.

It's not that I don't like talking with you, I do, I love it—it's just that I get so distracted. Sometimes when I'm praying I hear the dryer buzzer go off and think about all the wrinkles, or the light shines just right on the kitchen floor and I can see, well frankly, you don't want to know what I can see. Anyway, there's so much to do and I feel more comfortable being Martha than Mary. Martha's so practical, so matter-of-fact, a "let's get the job over and done with" kind of gal. I've always felt like a doer, not a pray-er, but lately I hear others around me talking about prayer as if it's as active as pulling weeds at a church work day. And there are so many things out of my control right now that I can't fix by myself, or even come close to fixing. Maybe I've done things backward all these years by thinking that prayer was the last resort, something to do when there was nothing else to do. Maybe the distractions have kept me from the real action.

So here I am ready to get started, hoping you'll help me through. There's a lot I don't understand, but I've got to get started somewhere. Oh, and one more thing. I feel pretty guilty about all the times I should have prayed but didn't for some reason or another (I've fallen asleep a few times when I was praying. Well actually, I've fallen asleep a lot—but I guess you know that too). I've decided that guilt won't accomplish much so I'm giving myself one more minute to feel bad and then I'm moving on.

Is this time all right with you? I think it'll work for me too. I won't run the dryer, and I'll turn off the light in the kitchen.

Love you, Ingrid

4. Jesus Balanced Private and Shared Praying

Jesus prayed alone, but he also prayed with others. Our relationship with God is personal but not private, and Jesus balanced the personal and the community aspects of prayer. He not only urges us to get alone to pray but also encourages us to pray with others: "Again, truly I tell you, if two of you agree on earth about anything you ask, it will be done for you by my Father in heaven" (Mt 18:19). Praying with the people of God was foundational to the worship of the Jewish people, and Jesus underscores Isaiah's teaching by reminding us that the temple was to be a house of prayer for the nations (Mk 11:17). It is no accident that the Lord's Prayer begins not with "*My* Father," but with "*Our* Father."

Jesus practices what he teaches: "Jesus took with him Peter and John and James, and went up on the mountain to pray" (Lk 9:28 par. Mt 17:1 and Mk 9:2).[4] Luke 9:18 strikes an explicit balance between praying alone and praying with others: "Once when Jesus was praying alone, with only the disciples near him, he asked them, 'Who do the crowds say that I am?'" People were present with Jesus while he prayed after his baptism, and his prayer is recorded because others were there and heard him pray.

All of this should counteract a "me and Jesus only" approach to God. Jesus balances the "me" and the "us" of praying. He criticizes the Pharisee who distances himself from others in his prayers, and the spatial picture Jesus paints shows the arrogance that attends an individualistic approach: "Two men went up to the temple to pray, one a Pharisee and the other a tax collector. The Pharisee, *standing by himself*, was praying thus, 'God, I thank you that I am not like other people: thieves, rogues, adulterers, or even like this tax collector'" (Lk 18:10-11, emphasis added).

It strikes me that "standing by himself" is an intentional jab at an individualistic approach to God. This story tells us to avoid spiritual pride when we are praying by joining with others. When we pray with others, we realize our own weaknesses and needs, and we find the encouragement and the grace that God has placed in the people who make up the body of Christ (see 1 Cor 12). I have found that joining with Jesus' people in small-group prayer encourages growth in my private prayer life.

5. Jesus Prayed Before Meals

It is very easy to establish a pattern of praying five times a day. If we pray after we get up and before we go to bed, as well as before each meal, we have developed a rhythm for praying several times a day.

Jesus prayed before meals, a common Jewish practice. He "blessed" the meal he was about to eat: "Taking the five loaves and the two fish, he looked up to heaven, and blessed and broke the loaves, and gave them to his disciples to set before the people" (Mk 6:41; see also Mk 8:7; 14:22; Lk 24:30). In the Lord's Prayer he teaches us to ask for our daily bread, and when he sat down to eat he gave thanks for God's daily provision.

In our family we share responsibility for praying at meals. Sometimes it is spontaneous, and sometimes we join in a blessing we pray together such as "God is great, God is good, let us thank him for our food." (This prayer was especially helpful when our children were first learning to talk.) Now a favorite is to sing to the tune of the doxology,

> Be present at our table, Lord.
> Be here and everywhere adored.
> Your mercies bless and grant that we
> May strengthened for your service be. Amen.

Prayer becomes a regular invitation to Christ to sit with us when we eat, and it encourages us to include Christ in our sharing around the table.

How would Jesus handle prayer before meals in our restaurant-loving society? Clearly, he would pray before meals, but he would not draw attention to himself by praying ostentatiously. It is possible to say a prayer with eyes open and lips closed. Often a booth allows us the humble opportunity for spoken prayers.

6. Jesus Gave Thanks

Jesus gave thanks in prayer (for example, Mt 11:25 par. Lk 10:21). It is only good manners to return thanks for a kindness done to us. Thanksgiving is essential to prayer, since all that we are, all that we have and all that we receive comes from our gracious God. To fail to give thanks reflects on the condition of our relationship with God. If we are not thanking God, we are probably unaware of God's merciful and generous provision.

Jesus encountered our human propensity to forget God's grace. In a village north of Jerusalem he healed ten lepers, but only one praised "God with a loud voice." He fell before Jesus and thanked him, grateful for deliverance from a condition that not only plagued him physically but also isolated him socially. Jesus affirms him even as he confronts the thanklessness of the others with, "Were not ten made clean? But the other nine, where are they?" (Lk 17:11-19). Jesus gave thanks when he prayed and considered it a normal response to a loving God who answers our requests. Jesus had learned gratitude in prayer from the Psalms. "O give thanks to the LORD, for he is good; for his steadfast love endures forever" (Ps 106:1; see also Ps 107:1; 118:1; 138:1). We need to remember and to be reminded of God's goodness and greatness. Thanksgiving is essential for remembering who God is and what God has done (for example, 1 Kings 8:23-24; 2 Kings 19:15-19; Is 37:16-20).

7. Jesus Sang Some Prayers

Jesus learned from his heritage the power of singing some prayers. Jesus prayed and sang from the Psalms, the Jewish book of hymns and prayers. For example, on his last journey to the Mount of Olives Jesus sang psalms with the disciples (Mk 14:26 par. Mt 26:30). This prayer practice was adopted by the early church: "Be filled with the Spirit, as you sing psalms and hymns and spiritual songs among yourselves, singing and making melody to the Lord in your hearts, giving thanks to God the Father at all times and for everything" (Eph 5:18-20).

Sung prayers are a powerful prayer tool. Singing causes our bodies, our minds and our spirits to work in concert, being caught up in the experience of beautiful music. For those of us with overly active minds, singing seizes our attention and helps focus our thoughts. But if all we do is pray while a CD plays, we run the risk of pushing out prayer in favor of listening to enjoyable music. Then we are sure to miss the still, small voice of God that comes in the quiet times. Even so, Jesus sang some prayers, and our prayer life is enhanced when we access the gift of music and beauty that the Creator God built into creation.

8. Jesus Prayed Before Making Important Decisions

It was Jesus' practice to pray before making important decisions. The more important the decision, the longer he prayed about it. For example, the most critical decision Jesus faced was choosing his disciples—followers who would receive and pass on his instructions as well as found his church. They were essential to Jesus' mission and purpose on earth. Luke describes Jesus' actions before he made this strategic decision: "Now during those days he went out to the mountain to pray; and he spent the night in prayer to God. And when day came, he called his disciples and chose twelve of them, whom he also named apostles" (Lk 6:12-13).

Luke does not tell us exactly what happened in that night of prayer, simply that Jesus spent the night in prayerful preparation for perhaps the most important decision of his ministry. Did Jesus hear names of specific people on that mountain? Did he have a long list of candidates, which he had to whittle down to twelve? Did he know at that time what selecting Judas would entail? Peter? None of these questions are answered. All we are told is that Jesus spent the night in prayer.

Why was praying before a decision so important to Jesus? The reason is simple: he wanted to be in tune with God's will and purpose (Jn 4:34). It is easy to go through life making all sorts of decisions without considering what God may want in each of those circumstances. When we look at two of the clearest records of our decisions, our checkbooks and our calendars, it is readily apparent whose will and whose glory we have sought with the balance of our time, money and energy. Praying before decisions, on the other hand, reorients us toward God. What does God want for me? Why have I been placed in this circumstance? What gifts has God called me to exercise? What is God's mind and wisdom about this opportunity?

9. Jesus Prayed for His Disciples

Jesus prayed for the ones he was most invested in. His practice affirms our natural inclination to pray for those closest to us. Jesus' "high priestly prayer" for his disciples (Jn 17:9-26) echoes almost every element of the Lord's Prayer that he taught them to pray. His prayer can show us how to pray for others.

First, he prays for our perseverance as Christians. Many fall away, and so Jesus prays, "Protect them in your name" (Jn 17:11) and "protect them from the evil one" (Jn 17:15). He prays that we will run the race to the end, that we "may be with me where I am, to see my glory" (Jn 17:24).

Second, he prays for our unity. Twenty centuries of church history demonstrate the importance of this prayer. Jesus prays "so that they may be one" (Jn 17:11, 21-23). This is essential for the internal dynamics of any particular congregation of Christians. Unity improves the witness of every congregation, enabling its members to pull together for God's glory.

Third, he prays for our spiritual satisfaction. He asks that they "may have my joy made complete in themselves" (Jn 17:13). Struggle and suffering attend the faithful Christian life, and this makes Jesus' prayer for joy that much more poignant. As Augustine is often quoted as saying, we are restless until we find our rest in God. Jesus prays for the full fruits of that essential relationship in our lives.

Fourth, he prays for our growth in personal holiness. "Sanctify them in [or by] the truth; your word is truth" (Jn 17:17). We have not yet arrived where we should be. We are declared holy through Christ's saving work (imputed righteousness), but we are becoming more and more holy through the cleansing and the character development of the Holy Spirit (imparted righteousness). Thus Jesus prays for the process of sanctification that we all undergo.

Finally, he prays for our witness to those who are not yet Christians. His prayer is that we will fulfill our marching orders to go into all the world to make disciples of all nations (Mt 28:16-20; Acts 1:8). We are blessed to be a blessing to others. So he prays, "I ask not only on behalf of these, but also on behalf of those who will believe in me through their word" (Jn 17:20).

10. Jesus Still Prays for Us

The most encouraging news to be found in the Bible about prayer is that Jesus has made it his continuing purpose to pray for me and for you: he "always lives to intercede for them [his disciples]" (Heb 7:25, my translation). Knowing my own faltering faithfulness, I am greatly encouraged to know that when I do not pray or do not know how to pray, Jesus stands in the gap making petitions to God on my behalf. He is faithful when we falter, and he always knows how to pray as he should:

"Likewise the Spirit helps us in our weakness; for we do not know how to pray as we ought, but that very Spirit intercedes with sighs too deep for words. And God, who searches the heart, knows what is the mind of the Spirit, because the Spirit intercedes for the saints according to the will of God" (Rom 8:26-27).

Jesus' example in prayer is crowned by this final observation. Prayer is about an intimate relationship with God that continues on into eternity. Jesus "lives" for that relationship with God and keeps you and me in mind as he communes with the Father. When we pray, we join a prayer meeting that Jesus is already leading on our behalf. He does not call us to be expert pray-ers. The important thing is that we, like Jesus, make this conversational relationship with God a central part of our lives.

Questions for Further Reflection

1. Are you confident that God will hear and answer your prayers? Why or why not?

2. Which side of the prayer-action equation do you need work on? Are you more likely to "pray as though it all depends on God" or to "act as though it all depends on you?"

3. Do you pray more often when you are alone or when you are with others? Why?

4. Consider your meal-time prayers. Do you ever struggle with the routine of praying before meals?

5. Do you have any memorized prayers that you sing or pray? When are they most helpful? (For example, when I feel stressed, the Serenity Prayer is very helpful: "God grant me the serenity to accept the things I cannot change, the courage to change the things I can, and the wisdom to know the difference.")

6. Are you facing any decisions right now that would benefit

from intensive prayer on your part?

7. What new or struggling Christians in your life would benefit from special prayer right now?

8. What things are you grateful for? Have you thanked God for them lately?

3

Jesus &
Jewish Prayer

I n *chapter two we noted that Jesus' example of prayer is a great* encouragement for my daughters and me, as well as many others. Some, however, may dismiss Jesus' example with the thought, "Well, that worked for Jesus, but he is God. It doesn't help a mere mortal like me!" Jesus was God, and yet he needed to pray. There are at least two reasons for Jesus to pray: (1) he was truly human and (2) he prayed as an example for our instruction.

Why Jesus Prayed

1. Jesus needed to pray as one who was truly human. Christians through the ages have acknowledged a great central mystery of our faith: one God is known in three distinct persons—Father, Son and Holy Spirit. Together they are one God, but they are distinct in their roles and their characters. This is the doctrine of the Trinity. When Jesus prays to the Father, he demonstrates that he has a different role as the second person of the Trinity. God the Father provides at the request of God the Son.

When Jesus walked on the earth, he limited himself to the restrictions that apply to all human beings. The clearest example of Jesus' humanity is his death. As a human being, Jesus was subject to the laws of coercion and execution, and he allowed his blood to be shed on the cross. He chose to limit himself in human flesh for a time in order to save the world. As the apostle Paul writes, "Though he was in the form of God, [he] did not regard equality with God as something to be exploited, but emptied himself, taking the form of a slave, being born in human likeness. And being found in human form, he humbled himself and became obedient to the point of death—even death on a cross" (Phil 2:6-8).

Jesus' execution shows his self-imposed limitations. As a fully human person, Jesus' practice of prayer is sincere and necessary. Like you and me, he *needed* to pray as a human being because he was dependent on God in the same ways that you and I are. Indeed, his prayers were potent because of his humble heart: "He was heard because of his reverent submission" (Heb 5:7).

2. He prayed to show us how. Jesus prayed in order to teach by example. When we acknowledge that "Christianity is not so much taught as caught," we are acknowledging a teaching principle that goes all the way back to Jesus. This is why Jesus calls disciples by saying, "Follow me" (Mt 9:9). The word *disciple* means "learner." Those who follow Jesus learn from him. This is precisely how he taught so much in such a compact period of time. He modeled what he taught, and he taught what he modeled. If you have ever done any teaching, you know how powerful modeling is as a method of instruction. It works in every aspect of life: a teacher works out a math problem on the board, a tennis coach demonstrates the proper way to hit a forehand, a coworker shows the quickest method of accessing e-mail—and the master Pray-er teaches how to pray.

Luke tells us that the Lord's Prayer was given to us as Jesus "was praying in a certain place, and after he had finished, one of his disciples said to him, 'Lord, teach us to pray, as John taught his disciples' " (Lk 11:1). Jesus modeled prayer, they observed his practice and asked him questions, and then Jesus gave them instruction to clarify his example. Jesus prayed because he needed to as the Son who was dependent on the Father and because he was called to as the one whom God sent to teach us about the ways of God.

Jewish Prayer and the Human Jesus

When we accept that Jesus became fully human, then we understand that he became fully Jewish, adopting the customs and speaking the language of the people he was born among. It is no surprise that his prayers reflect the Judaism of his day. Much of what Jesus teaches us about prayer he learned from the Hebrew Scriptures and from the prayer practices of his Jewish heritage. One of the first things we learn from Jesus is that he did not invent prayer. Rather, he stands hand in hand with the Jewish people of God in a long tradition of prayer, which he refines and passes on.

Prayer was foundational to the worship of the Jewish people, as the importance of the temple in Jerusalem indicates. The temple was the center of Jewish worship in Jesus' day and was designed by God to be "a house of prayer." The Jewish prophet Isaiah taught this (Is 56:7), and Jesus reaffirmed it when he himself went to the temple to pray. But Jesus found that the temple's purpose had been corrupted by entrepreneurs who were using the temple courts for financial gain. He cried out the words of Isaiah, "It is written, 'My house shall be called a house of prayer,' " and then he added the chastisement of Jeremiah, "but you are making it a den of robbers" (Mt 21:13 par. Mk 11:17 and Lk 19:46; see Jer 7:11).[1] Jews like Jesus knew that the temple was for prayer, not profit.

Jesus' spirituality was solidly rooted in Jewish piety. Jewish devotion had three pillars: prayer, alms giving and fasting. As a Jew, Jesus naturally treats these three together in Matthew 6, giving instructions on prayer and the Lord's Prayer in the middle of his instructions about alms giving and fasting. By treating prayer among the big three in Jewish spirituality, Jesus firmly establishes his views on prayer within the practices of the Jewish people of God.

Some Christians have forgotten this great heritage of prayer. One of the earliest Christian heresies was Marcion's second-century attempt to draw a sharp distinction between Christianity and its Jewish antecedents. Marcion wanted Christians to reject the Old Testament, as well as anything in the New Testament that reflected its Jewish roots. Fortunately, the early Christian church rejected Marcion's views and established faith in Christ as being congruent with the long-standing Jewish understanding of the ways of God. Likewise, Jesus' prayers stand in continuity with the ancient Jewish heritage of prayer. Neglect of the Jewish aspect of Jesus' prayers greatly impoverishes our understanding of prayer that has been revealed to the people of God through the ages.

Another factor that can lead us to overlook the importance of Jesus' Jewish prayer heritage is our contemporary emphasis on the "new and improved," by which we tend to identify the older as the inferior. Not Jesus. He understood prayer as something that was learned and taught by the people of God throughout the ages. This tradition lent it credibility. The heritage of prayer preserves God's dealings with people. In this sense, Jesus' practice of prayer was grounded in the history of God's interactions with people, was rooted in experience, and was tested over time.

Theologian Oscar Cullmann states simply and correctly, "New Testament prayer is rooted in the Old Testament."[1] Jesus' own example shows us that we should not speak of "Christian prayer" without realizing that it is "biblical prayer." To study Jesus' prayers requires us to examine what he learned about prayer in his Jewish family and surroundings.

Jewish Practices That Jesus Adopted

Jesus' prayer life included several distinctively Jewish characteristics. He adopted these practices as any Jew of his day would have.

1. Jesus addressed God as "Father" in prayer. Jesus addressed God as "Father" in his prayers and taught his disciples to do the same (see Mt 6; 7:11; 18:19; 26:39, 42; Mk 11:25; Lk 11:2; Jn 4:23; 14:16).[2] This was the custom of pious Jewish Palestinians.[3] In Isaiah the people cry out to God, "For you are our Father, though Abraham does not know us and Israel does not acknowledge us; you, O LORD, are our father; our Redeemer from of old is your name" (Is 63:16). "Yet, O LORD, you are our Father; we are the clay, and you are our potter; we are all the work of your hand" (Is 64:8).

Consider other prayers from first-century Palestinian Jews that address God as Father:

> O Lord, Father and Master of my life, do not abandon me to their designs, and do not let me fall because of them! (Sirach 23:1)

> O Lord, Father and God of my life, do not give me haughty eyes. (Sirach 23:4)

> We are considered by him as something base, and he avoids our ways as unclean; he calls the last end of the righteous happy, and boasts that God is his father. Let us see if his words are true, and let us test what will happen at the end of his life; for if the righteous man is God's child, he will help him, and will deliver him from the

hand of his adversaries. (Wisdom 2:16-18)

But it is your providence, O Father, that steers its course, because you have given it a path in the sea, and a safe way through the waves. (Wisdom 14:3)

Thus it is the Jewish Jesus praying the first words of the Lord's Prayer in the language of his heart: "Our Father in heaven." He could just as well be Solomon praying to dedicate the temple or Nehemiah or Ezra calling out to the God of heaven (1 Kings 8:30, 34, 36, 39, 43, 49; Neh 1:4; 9:6).[4]

2. *Jesus opened his eyes and lifted his hands when he prayed.* Like other Jews of his day, Jesus prayed with his eyes open: "He looked up to heaven and said, 'Father'" (Jn 17:1; Lk 18:11-13; Ps 121:1). Like other Jews, Jesus lifted his hands to pray (Lk 24:50), as did the early Christians (1 Tim 2:8). There are many examples from the Old Testament, of which Psalm 63:4 is one: "So I will bless you as long as I live; I will lift up my hands and call on your name" (Ex 9:29; 17:12; 1 Kings 8:22, 38; 2 Chron 6:12; Neh 8:6; Ps 28:2; 44:20). Like other Jews, Jesus sometimes laid his hands on those he prayed for (Mt 19:13; Mk 6:5; 10:16; Lev 4:15; Num 8:10; Deut 34:9).

3. *Jesus sang and prayed the Psalms.* On one occasion we find Jesus "singing a hymn" with his disciples (*hymnēsantes,* Mk 14:26 par. Mt 26:30), and this hymn probably came from the book of Psalms.[5] The most striking example of Jesus' praying from the Psalms occurred on the cross when he cried out, "My God, my God, why have you forsaken me?" (Mk 15:34 par. Mt 27:46). These are the opening words of Psalm 22. In typically Jewish manner, Jesus "prays" this psalm to express his feelings to God. We are left to wonder if he intended to pray all the way to the more comforting words of Psalm 23, "The LORD is my shepherd."

Those of us who come from low-church traditions of prayer and worship may have a hard time appreciating this part of Jesus' prayer life. Maybe we have thought or we have been taught that "reading prayers" is for those who do not really know how to pray or do not really have a personal relationship with God. Yet we allow ourselves to sing other people's prayers as songs. So how can we reject praying these same prayers without music as somehow "unspiritual" or ritualistic? We begin to understand this aspect of Jewish prayer when we feel close to God while singing a prayer that someone else has written. If we keep our minds open, we can have this same positive experience when we make someone else's prayers a guide for our own prayers. Modeling, after all, is Jesus' style of instruction.

4. Jesus prayed early in the morning and late in the evening. Mark remembers Jesus' morning routine: "In the morning, while it was still very dark, he got up and went out to a deserted place, and there he prayed" (Mk 1:35). Matthew reminds us that Jesus prayed in the evening also (Mt 14:23). Presumably, Jesus and other Jews learned this practice from the book of Psalms:

> Listen to the sound of my cry, my King and my God, for to you I pray. O LORD, in the morning you hear my voice; in the morning I plead my case to you, and watch. (Ps 5:2-3)

> Evening and morning and at noon I utter my complaint and moan, and he will hear my voice. (Ps 55:17)

> Daniel . . . continued . . . to get down on his knees three times a day to pray to his God and praise him. (Dan 6:10)

The last two passages refer to the habit of many Jews who prayed three times a day. We can only suppose that this was Jesus' habit as well. Written at the turn of the first Christian century, *Didache* 8.2 instructs Christians to pray the Lord's Prayer three times a day, and it may well be that this practice was derived from Jesus himself.

5. The Lord's Prayer contains some very Jewish elements. The Lord's

Prayer, recorded in Matthew 6 and Luke 11, is rooted in Jewish liturgical prayers. The first half of this prayer in particular is reminiscent of the Jewish Kaddish prayers (*kaddish* is Aramaic for "holy"). The Lord's Prayer was used in the early church in exactly the same way that "The Eighteen Benedictions," a Jewish prayer from this period, was used in contemporary synagogues. In fact, the two were similar in several respects. Both were used as an outline for prayer; the wording in both was flexible; both followed the same form—praise-petition-praise; both were used for congregational and private prayer; both were customarily prayed three times a day.[6] There are several scholarly studies that compare the Lord's Prayer and its Jewish antecedents, and we shall discuss these features further in the chapters that follow.[7] The Lord's Prayer is key evidence that Jesus' prayer practice, even the content of his prayers, is firmly rooted in his Jewish heritage.

What Jesus Learned from Negative Examples

Even though Jesus' prayers are very Jewish, there were some prayer practices that he rejected and specifically taught his disciples to reject. Jesus learned by observing the negative examples of others. I have already mentioned Jesus' confrontation at the temple, where the business practices of some opportunists showed disrespect for the temple's primary purpose—to be a place of prayer for all the nations (Mk 11:17 par. Mt 21:13 and Lk 19:46).

Jesus' teaching on prayer and piety in Matthew 6 is framed directly against religious practices that he wants his disciples to reject. Three times he tells them not to be like the "hypocrites" who practice their alms giving, prayer and fasting "so that they may be praised by others" (v. 2), "so that they may be seen by others" (v. 5) or "so as to show others that they are fasting" (v. 16). Perhaps we have all known persons who seem to think that acting "spiritual" will cause others to think well of them. Jesus roundly condemns this superficial spirituality and wants us to know that prayer is a matter of the heart, not appearances. God pays attention to heartfelt alms giving, prayer and fasting, because "your Father who sees in secret will reward you" (vv. 4, 6, 18).

But Jesus targets more than the misguided practices of some spiritual phonies he had observed in the synagogue. He also criticizes the repetition and babbling that he observed in the Greco-Roman cults: "When you are praying, do not heap up empty phrases as the Gentiles do; for they think that they will be heard because of their many words. Do not be like them, for your Father knows what you need before you ask him" (Mt 6:7-8). But the Gentiles did not have a lock on long prayers, as Jesus also criticizes scribes who were long-winded and hungry for recognition: "They devour widows' houses and for the sake of appearance say long prayers. They will receive the greater condemnation" (Mk 12:40 par. Lk 20:47). Against this, Jesus asserts that God is not manipulated by the appearance of piety but responds to straightforward and simple speech. Good relationships require honest communication, and Jesus teaches that "true worshipers will worship the Father in spirit and truth, for the Father seeks such as these to worship him" (Jn 4:23).

Another target of Jesus' criticism was self-righteousness and spiritual arrogance in prayer. With a parable he confronts the religious elite, "who trusted in themselves that they were righteous and regarded others with contempt" (Lk 18:9):

> Two men went up to the temple to pray, one a Pharisee and the other a tax collector. The Pharisee, standing by himself, was praying thus, "God, I thank you that I am not like other people: thieves, rogues, adulterers, or even like this tax collector." (Lk 18:10-11)

This smug self-righteousness was repugnant to Jesus. But he praised the humility and the contrite spirit of the tax collector who could not even raise his eyes to heaven because of his guilt. He beat his breast and prayed, "God, be merciful to me, a sinner!" (18:13). And Jesus concludes, "I tell you, this man went down to his home justified rather than the other; for all who exalt themselves will be humbled, but all who humble themselves will be exalted" (18:14). Indeed, Jesus' popularity with the masses was largely due to his criticism of the spiritual elite and his teaching about the God who is accessible to the common, penitent person. When we pray, we should pray with humble hearts and an honest recognition of our sinfulness before a holy God.

Yet Jesus found good to reclaim from the bad in the prayer practices of his day. His ability to retrieve the wheat from the chaff sets an example for those of us who may have had negative encounters with prayer or with someone's notions about prayer. Jesus teaches us to glean what is good and then move beyond the negative examples of others. Let me give one personal example. A long time ago I had a bad experience with "name it and claim it," or "confidence teaching," prayer. In the version of this teaching that I heard, the emphasis was not on God's sovereignty or our dependence, but on the boldness and confidence that we express when we pray. Persons who pray boldly are assured that they *will* get what they ask for. Those who do not receive are doubters or have some unconfessed sin in their lives. (I even heard it was wrong to pray "your will be done," since this is supposedly a subtle way of expressing a lack of confidence in one's prayers.) This teaching, as I heard it, seemed to shift the power and glory from God to the pray-er and portrayed God as a very cruel and calculating healer. If a cancer victim does not find healing, it is due to unconfessed sin or a lack of faith. This teaching is heartless and reflects little of the merciful, tender and gracious character of our God.

But then I rejected this "confidence" distortion with my own "no-confidence" distortion. My prayers began to contain so many opt-out clauses and became so tentative and halting that for a long time I stopped praying about circumstances that seemed difficult or impossible. The overreaction that I experienced to this teaching impoverished my own praying. I allowed my negative experience of someone else's praying to weaken my own praying. But looking to Jesus' confidence in prayer has helped me overcome my negative experience, and I am continually encouraged by Jesus' faith to pray boldly, knowing that God is gracious and merciful, often answering our prayers just as we pray them.

We looked at Jesus' example of prayer in chapter two. In this chapter we considered the humility, Jewishness and uniqueness of Jesus' praying. In the seven chapters that follow we will focus on Jesus' magnum opus on prayer—the Lord's Prayer.

Questions for Further Reflection

1. How often do you pray? For how long? Is prayer a struggle or an opportunity for you? What expectations do you have for how much a Christian should pray? Is this expectation based on Scripture or on someone's opinion?

2. What negative experiences or reservations do you have about prayer? How can you avoid letting the pitfalls that you observe in others spoil bold prayer on your part?

3. When do you pray? What natural rhythms of the day can you use to enhance your prayer life?

4. What physical posture do you find most enhances your time of prayer? What are the advantages to kneeling? sitting? standing? folded hands? raised arms? closed eyes? open eyes?

5. Do you have favorite songs or recorded music that help you pray? What is it about the music or the words that you find helpful?

4

Praying the Lord's Prayer

Jesus' most famous instructions on prayer are given to us in the Lord's Prayer (Mt 6:9-13 par. Lk 11:2-4). The "Our Father" is prayed around the globe in virtually every language. The reason Christians pray this prayer is simple. The disciples requested, "Lord teach us to pray," and Jesus responded with the gift of this prayer, "When you pray, say: Father . . ." (Lk 11:1-2).

When I first began praying the Lord's Prayer as a teenager, some elements of it touched me deeply, while others remained a complete mystery. I could understand praying for God's will, though I had little notion of what I was asking for when I pleaded for God's kingdom to come. I understood my need to ask for forgiveness, but I had no idea what "hallowed be thy name" meant. Furthermore, the alien expressions of King James's English did not encourage me to find an intimate relationship with God.

I suspect that the compact nature of this prayer, combined

with the archaic English in which it is usually prayed, works to keep many of us from a full appreciation of the instruction that Jesus gives us in it. For many of us the Lord's Prayer has become a way of piling up meaningless words when we pray, which is ironic in view of Jesus' admonition "When you are praying, do not heap up empty phrases as the Gentiles do; for they think that they will be heard because of their many words" (Mt 6:7). The next several chapters unpack the rich meaning of this prayer, encourage us to pray it with more understanding and ease, address many of the questions and reservations that Christians have about this prayer, and apply the prayer instructions of the Lord's Prayer to the rest of our prayer lives.

Traditionally Christians have prayed the version that Matthew records. This practice goes back to the *Didache*—church instructions that were written just after the turn of the first Christian century. Below are the two versions of the Lord's Prayer—Matthew's and Luke's:

Matthew 6:9-13	Luke 11:2-4
Our Father in heaven,	Father,
hallowed be your name.	hallowed be your name.
Your kingdom come.	Your kingdom come.
Your will be done,	
on earth as it is in heaven.	
Give us this day our daily bread.	Give us each day our daily bread.
And forgive us our debts, as we also have forgiven our debtors.	And forgive us our sins, for we ourselves forgive everyone indebted to us.
And do not bring us to the time of trial,	And do not bring us to the time of trial.
but rescue us from the evil one.	

It is natural to wonder why we have two versions of this prayer. Is one original and the other a copy? Did Jesus give us two prayers, similar yet different? Did Matthew expand Luke's shorter version for his more Jewish audience? Or did Luke abbreviate Matthew's prayer for his more Hellenistic audience? What do we make, if anything, of these supposed abbreviations or expansions? Why did Matthew's version become the prayer of choice for the Christian church? These questions find only speculative responses.[1]

The Flexibility of Praying the Lord's Prayer

There is a key lesson that we can learn from the differences in these two versions, one that can help us as we seek to pray Jesus' way. This lesson is *flexibility*. Whether these are two prayers of Jesus or two adaptations of one prayer, the witness that they provide when taken together invites us to be flexible in our use of this prayer. Both Matthew and Luke were probably written down in the latter part of the first Christian century. Obviously Christians had not taken one version of the Lord's Prayer as *the* way to pray it. Comparing Luke with Matthew shows that the earliest Christians were adaptable in their use of the Lord's Prayer.

This is supported by what the early church fathers actually taught about how the Lord's Prayer should be used to direct our personal prayers. Tertullian, a Roman convert to Christianity, writes about the Lord's Prayer, "Jesus Christ our Lord has marked out for us disciples of the New Covenant a new outline of prayer."[2] Origen, a second-century teacher from northern Egypt, calls the Lord's Prayer the prayer "outlined" and "sketched out" by the Lord to teach us what we should pray about.[3] Origen goes on to summarize the four aspects of a prayer outline: praise, thanksgiving, confession and petition. Thus Origen is the first to derive from the Lord's Prayer the popular prayer outline often taught today through the acronym A.C.T.S.:

Adoration
Confession
Thanksgiving
Supplication[4]

We can see this flexibility in how the churches of Matthew and Luke were praying the prayer. Consider the opening address, for example. Matthew, shaping his Gospel for Jewish readers, uses the very familiar Jewish opening, "Our Father in heaven." Luke's simpler "Father" seems better suited to his Hellenistic audience, which would be unfamiliar with the Jewish etiquette of addressing God as the Father in heaven. Luke's adaptation and flexibility releases us to begin our prayers in familiar and flexible ways. Each of us tends to begin our conversation with God in a different way, and we should feel encouraged to be ourselves in prayer: "Dear God," "Creator God," "Lord Jesus," "Spirit of God," "Our gracious heavenly Father," "Lord"—the list goes on and on. We need not become anxious about the words we use to begin our prayers. But, as the Lord's Prayer shows, we should have immense respect for the One to whom we pray, regardless of the chosen form of address. When we approach the Lord's Prayer with an awareness of the two biblical versions, we are released to pray freely, always learning from Jesus how our freedom in prayer can be channeled and directed to God.

The Formality of Praying the Lord's Prayer
It commonly suggested that Jesus gave the Lord's Prayer *only* as an outline for prayer, not as a set formal prayer. Jesus' introduction to the prayer in Matthew 6:9 lends support to this approach, "Pray then in this way." Jesus emphasizes flexibility even as he discourages rigidity and repetition. In the chapters that follow we will explore using the Lord's Prayer as an outline to enhance our prayers as we expand the topics we pray about.

We should also not overlook the value of the Lord's Prayer as a set prayer. Jesus told his followers, "When you pray, *say* . . ." (Lk 11:2). He does not say, "Use the following words as an outline for what you will say." Rather, he simply tells them to say (Greek *legete*) these words in their prayers. By the time of the *Didache* in the early second century, Christians were being encouraged to pray the prayer three times a day, using the form we find in Matthew with the addition of the familiar doxology, "For thine is the kingdom and the power and the glory forever. Amen"(*Didache* 8.2). There are times when actually praying the words of the Lord's Prayer is beneficial, particularly when we use it in a gathered congregation to unite our prayers. This helps us make sense of the plural nature of the prayer: "*Our* Father . . . give *us* . . . forgive *us* . . . deliver *us*." We can benefit from praying the Lord's Prayer in the form it has been passed on to us, particularly if we have come to understand its rich meaning.

When we pray the Lord's Prayer word for word, we need to note that this is *the beginning place* of Jesus' instruction on prayer. This is not all Jesus taught about prayer, nor did he suggest that we should limit our prayers to a recitation of the Lord's Prayer. Rather, as a good teacher, Jesus provided a solid beginning place for learning to pray Jesus' way. It is very helpful, when we are beginning to pray, to follow someone else's example. Billy Graham always encourages those who come forward at his evangelistic meetings to follow his simple model for a "sinner's prayer." This prayer is not the only one that Graham prays or the only one that he thinks new converts should pray. Rather, he offers a model prayer as a starting place for those who are beginning a relationship with God but are not sure how to go about it.

When I learned to hit a forehand shot with my tennis racket, my first efforts were stiff imitations of my instructor's model. Later that foundation helped me learn the necessary discipline for adapting my own best form for my game. So it is with the Lord's Prayer.

Repetition of the Lord's Prayer does not necessarily make its words less meaningful. I have been saying "I love you" to my wife for over fourteen years. Obviously I did not originate that line. After being repeated for fourteen years, the words mean more, not less, both to me and to her. The meaning of "I love you" has deepened because our relationship has grown through demonstrations of caring for each other. These are not the only three words I say to her, but I do say these three often, and she appreciates my doing so. I think the same can be true for the Lord's Prayer. It is someone else's words, but the repetition of it—combined with a growing relationship with God—can come to mean more and more as time goes by. I am deeply appreciative to Jesus for giving this memorable prayer. It helps keep my other prayers from becoming narrow and self-centered.

However we pray the Lord's Prayer, we must do so from the heart, not mechanically. As Jesus announces, "But the hour is coming, and is now here, when the true worshipers will worship the Father in spirit and truth, for the Father seeks such as these to worship him" (Jn 4:23). In the chapters that follow, we shall explore the meaning of the Lord's Prayer line by line so that we can pray each part from the heart, in spirit and in truth.

Questions for Further Reflection

1. When was the last time you prayed the Lord's Prayer?

2. If you have not already done so, take some time and memorize the Lord's Prayer so that you can pray it wherever you are, whenever you would like to. The translation memorized by most English-speaking Christians is Matthew's version in King James English with an expanded ending from *Didache* 8.2:

Our Father who art in heaven,
hallowed be thy name.
Thy kingdom come.
Thy will be done,
on earth as it is in heaven.
Give us this day our daily bread.
Forgive us our trespasses [debts],
as we forgive [our debtors] those who trespass against us.
And lead us not into temptation,
but deliver us from evil.
[For thine is the kingdom and the power and the glory forever.
Amen.]

3. Which elements of the Lord's Prayer are the most meaningful for you?

4. Which elements of the Lord's Prayer are the least meaningful for you?

5. Are you more likely to pray the Lord's Prayer word for word or to use it as a guideline for more spontaneous praying? How can the other way of praying it enrich your prayer life?

5

Seeking God's Face in Prayer

Our Father in heaven,
hallowed be your name.
MATTHEW 6:9

My *children come to me for many reasons. In the middle of the* night they come running into my bedroom afraid, having had a bad dream. When they fall and scrape a knee, they come because they are hurt. Often they come with needs or wants: "Dad, can I have . . ." But the best times for me are when they simply want to be with me. They call out, "Dad, where are you?" and they come and sit with me. Maybe they talk and maybe they don't. We exchange affection and reassure each other of our love.

We come to God for the same reasons: fears, hurts, needs, wants, intimacy. These are all good reasons for coming to God, but Jesus teaches us to begin prayer by remembering who God is: "Our Father in heaven, hallowed be your name." Though there may be times when we rush to God in great need, Jesus teaches us to discipline ourselves to begin with the holy God who made us and gives us life and being. Jesus begins the Lord's

Prayer with a reminder of this precious relationship we have with God. We are a part of God's family, and we pray to the God of all nations who is over all people and all places: "Our Father in heaven." The asking comes later. We begin with a clear remembrance of the preciousness and sacredness of the One to whom we pray.

A friend pointed out to me that Jesus teaches us to seek the face of God first when we pray, not the hand of God. We do not begin prayer with a wish list. We begin with honoring the God to whom we pray and becoming fully aware of God's holiness and status over all the universe: "Our Father in heaven, may your holy name be honored." This is the first thing Jesus teaches us about prayer: begin prayer with God and God's concerns, not a shopping list of needs and wants. Seeking God's face in prayer requires that we understand our relationship with God through Christ.

A Special Relationship with God

Jesus' relationship with God was one of a kind, since Jesus was uniquely God's Son as the second person of the Trinity. As John puts it, Jesus "was also calling God his own Father, thereby making himself equal to God" (Jn 5:18). Jesus knew God in a way only he could since he was the incarnate bearer of God's divine nature. When we pray "Our Father" with Jesus, we do not imply that we share his divinity, but that we share his intimate family relationship with God. Jesus is God's child by nature, but we become God's children by spiritual adoption. The apostle Paul writes,

> For you did not receive a spirit of slavery to fall back into fear, but you have received a spirit of adoption. When we cry, "Abba! Father!" it is that very Spirit bearing witness with our spirit that we are children of God, and if children, then heirs, heirs of God and joint heirs with Christ. (Rom 8:15-17)

This special relationship is celebrated in the first two words of the Lord's Prayer, "Our Father"—powerful words of God's redeeming love. No matter what our family background, nationality or gender, we are invited into the family of the redeemed through faith in Jesus Christ. The Holy Spirit indwells us, a seal on the adoption papers that make us God's through Christ. Jesus begins the Lord's Prayer with an invitation to boldly claim our family connection with God. The phrase "Our Father in heaven" means that we belong to God and that he is ours.

Hallowing God's Name

"Hallowed be your name." The opening of the Lord's Prayer is very Jewish in how it addresses God, and it is this Jewish context that helps us understand the deep reverence that Jesus says must accompany our approach to God in prayer.[1] Jewish prayer practices suggest that "Our Father in heaven" was a common circumlocution for the holy name of God—a name that could not be uttered aloud, even in prayer. God's "name" is sacred and needs to be kept set apart, holy, "hallowed." This name was first revealed to Moses when he interrogated God in preparation for his return to deliver the Israelites from Egypt:

> But Moses said to God, "If I come to the Israelites and say to them, 'The God of your ancestors has sent me to you,' and they ask me, 'What is his name?' what shall I say to them?" God said to Moses, 'I AM WHO I AM." He said further, "Thus you shall say to the Israelites, 'I AM has sent me to you.' " God also said to Moses, "Thus you shall say to the Israelites, 'The LORD [Yahweh], the God of your ancestors, the God of Abraham, the God of Isaac, and the God of Jacob, has sent me to you':
>
> > This is my name forever,
> > and this my title for all generations." (Ex 3:13-15)

In later Jewish practice this name Yahweh, "the Name," was considered so special that it would be defiled by sinful lips even mentioning it. The sanctity of "the Name" is protected in the third commandment, "You shall not make wrongful use of the name of the LORD [Yahweh] your God, for the LORD will not acquit anyone who misuses his name" (Ex 20:7). To avoid misusing the Name, it was common practice to use a synonym such as "the Name" or "Adonai" (Lord) to avoid being guilty of misusing "Yahweh."

The Lord's Prayer thus begins with our sense of belonging (*"Our* Father") to the God of ancient Israel, whose very name is sacred. We come into God's presence remembering that God deserves our complete respect, our deepest awe and our submissive deference, a response from us that no other being can command. God—who is over all, who delivered the Israelites out of absolute captivity in Egypt—is the holy God we address in prayer.

When we pray this first request, we are praying for several things. First, we pray that *we* will be sincere in our prayer and worship. "Hallowed be your name" is a prayer for our devotional life itself. We petition God not to let our prayers turn into mere ritual and rambling words without heartfelt commitment. The prophets and priests prayed this long before Jesus (Lev 22:32; Is 29:23; Ezek 36:20-23). We ask that God remain the holy and captivating center of our lives and consciousness so that when we pray our talking *with God* does not degenerate into talking *about God,* so that we never use God's name in an empty way, reciting prayers we do not really mean. "Hallowed be your name" is a request that God keep us from distractions when we pray, since, "generally speaking, in any prayer distraction leads to a devaluation."[2]

Second, "hallowed be your name" is a prayer for worldwide missions and our own personal evangelism, "Where I cause my name to be remembered" (Ex 20:24). This is a prayer for our personal relational network as well as any other place in the world where God's name is not honored, a prayer that those who ignore God will come to honor God's presence in their lives. We ask for not-yet Christians to become aware of God's presence and holiness and goodness. Jesus prays similarly in John 17:6, "I have made your name known to those whom you gave me from the world."

Third, "hallowed be your name" is a prayer for preachers and teachers and what they declare about God: "God, keep their tongues from saying anything flippant when they attach your authority to their words." We pray that those who speak God's Word will faithfully reflect what God has revealed in Scripture. As Jesus says in John 7:18, "Those who speak on their own seek their own glory; but the one who seeks the glory of him who sent him is true, and there is nothing false in him."

Fourth, when we pray "hallowed be your name" we are praying for ourselves and for all believers that we may live up to our "family name" and honor God with our lives. As Christians, we live in glass houses, and others observe us and know whose children we are. God's reputation is more intertwined with our own than we would sometimes like to admit. We have a God to honor by how we conduct our lives, and so we seek God's help in living up to our calling. We pray, "Our Father in heaven, help us to honor your name"[3] by how we live and act and relate.

What About Praying to "Daddy"?

Jesus begins the Lord's Prayer with a solemn and respectful approach to God, which is quite different from the extremely popular and widespread misunderstanding that Jesus taught us to pray to God as our "daddy." This mistake is repeated over and over again in books and sermons. It goes like this: "Jesus taught us to pray to *abba*, the Aramaic word for 'daddy.'" This comment is twice wrong, but it is widely believed and is deeply ingrained in popular theology of prayer.

First, the word *abba* is not used in the Lord's Prayer. Matthew uses the Greek for "our Father" (*Pater hēmōn;* Luke simply has "Father," *Pater*). "Our Father" was commonly known in the prayers of Palestinian Judaism of the first century, making it just as likely that Jesus prayed abhinu ("our father") as *abba* ("father"). It is misguided to build a case on *abba* when it is not certain that this is the original word Jesus used. There is only one place in the Gospels where it is recorded that Jesus prays to God as *abba*—his prayer in Gethsemane (Mk 14:36, *Abba ho patēr;* see Gal 4:6; Rom 8:15). To say that Jesus taught us to pray to our *abba* is not textually grounded.

Second, if *abba* is behind this text (and it may well be), it is most unlikely that it should be translated "daddy." *Abba* is better translated "dear father." "Daddy" was popularized as a translation by Joachim Jeremias in the late 1960s, but his style of argument was flawed, and he later called his own approach "a piece of inadmissible naïveté." Jeremias recanted, and other scholars have refuted his earlier notion. But many preachers and writers have clung to Jeremias's misguided earlier view that *abba* is the chatter of a small child.[4] In a tour de force, Oxford linguist James Barr has shown that Jeremias was mistaken in this now widespread view. *Abba* is best translated with "more a solemn, responsible, adult address to Father."[5] As Barr shows, if "daddy" had been meant, there were Greek words for it. But Matthew, Luke, Mark and Paul did not choose from among those Greek possibilities (*papas, pappas, pappias, pappidion*). In the three places where *abba* appears in the New Testament, it is immediately translated by a very formal Greek phrase, literally "the Father" (*ho patēr;* Mk 14:36; Gal 4:6; Rom 8:15).[6]

Furthermore, the context of the Lord's Prayer supports a

more solemn understanding of how Jesus teaches us to address God. The first full sentence of the Lord's Prayer does not take us down the road of childish and individualistic intimacy with God, "my daddy," as we would expect if Jeremias's earlier view were correct. Jesus teaches us to focus on the holiness of God's name and character, and this had to mean for Jesus and his original hearers a focus on the solemn name that God gave to Moses—Yahweh. Jesus teaches us to pray not "my daddy" but "*our* Father, the one in heaven.*"*

We begin prayer with awesome respect for our holy God: "may your holy name be honored." The emphasis is on God's holiness and transcendence, as the second part of the verse clarifies. Prayer, like wisdom, begins with respectful awe for the Lord. Suggesting that we should pray to our "daddy," in addition to being textually unfounded, overlooks the profound emphasis Jesus places on respect for God in the opening of the Lord's Prayer.

God's Loving Parental Care for Us

Even though *abba* does not mean "daddy," it does remind us that God prizes intimacy with us in prayer. We belong in the throne room of grace, and God is delighted to receive us each time we come. The deep reverence for God with which prayer begins does not minimize the tender relationship God desires with us. We learn from Jesus' teaching and example (not from the word *abba*) that reverence for God is mixed with intimacy; the call to obey God's authority is balanced by the promise of God's mercy and forgiveness. The image of a father in the ancient world usually carried connotations of obedience, provision and mercy. It is no surprise that the Lord's Prayer develops all three: (1) obedience—"your kingdom come, your will be done," (2) provision—"give us this day our daily bread" and (3) mercy—"forgive us our debts, deliver us." Jesus teaches us through the Lord's Prayer and elsewhere that a relationship with God combines respect with intimacy, obedience and forgiveness.

We are known intimately by God. The psalmist tells us that God knows "when I sit down and when I rise up" (Ps 139:2). Jesus reminds us that God has a tender understanding of each of us, since "even the hairs of your head are all counted" (Mt 10:30). It is significant that little children came to Jesus. Far from being second-class citizens, women, children and slaves were not citizens at all. Thus it comes as no surprise that the disciples tried to turn the children away. What is surprising is that Jesus used children to model God's approach to each of us. We know we are not worthy to come to God, but Jesus' words to his disciples constitute an everlasting invitation to us: " 'Let the little children come to me; do not stop them; for it is to such as these that the kingdom of God belongs. Truly I tell you, whoever does not receive the kingdom of God as a little child will never enter it.' And he took them up in his arms, laid his hands on them, and blessed them" (Mk 10:14-16 par. Mt 19:14-15 and Lk 18:15-17).

Jesus tells another amazing story about God's tender love for us. The parable of the prodigal son is actually the story of the prodigal father (Lk 15:11-32). The word *prodigal* means "lavish." When the son who has squandered his entire inheritance in the fast lane comes home, his father runs to him and envelops him in a fatherly embrace. It is the father who is extravagant. He kills the fatted calf and throws a huge homecoming party for his newly found child. The prodigal father is a vivid portrait of God's character. Like the prodigal father, "God calls us to stop hiding and come openly to Him."[7] God still runs to prodigal children when we come limping home, and mercy triumphs over judgment.

With the phrase "Our Father" Jesus invites us into a personal intimacy with God that emphasizes our childlike trust. He does not teach that God is an abstract concept or that God is a remote deity who abandons us to speculations such as "If God knows everything, then why mention something in prayer?" or "If God is sovereign, then our wills and requests have no place in the scheme of things." A distant relationship with God invites "paralysis by analysis" and tends to leave us prayerless. Rather, Jesus teaches us to approach God as one who loves us dearly and cares deeply about our concerns and our lives. Because God knows us intimately, and because we have been adopted as beloved children, we are encouraged to pour out our hearts to our heavenly Father.

My daughter has sometimes approached me with, "I want to ask you something, but I'm afraid to because I know you'll say no." Reminding her that she really doesn't know how to read my mind, I encourage her to make her request, and she is often surprised to find that she has misjudged me. Prayer can be just like that. We become paralyzed before God when we never get beyond the analyzing to the asking. God surely wants to say to us, "Express yourself to me. I want to be in a relationship with you. I want to know you and to be known by you. Trust me, go ahead and ask. I am your loving God."

When *Father* Is a Dirty Word

We cannot end this chapter without considering the feelings of those for whom the word *father* conjures up a negative image that hinders their prayers. We live in a day and age when our use of language has undergone radical changes. The words *he* and *men* were once used to refer either to males or to all people regardless of gender. But this is no longer acceptable. To refer to all people, we say or write *humanity*. The word *men* is used to refer to adult males only. The main reason for making this distinction is the consensus view that language reflects thinking. The unchallenged male perspective traditionally expressed through the English language directly mirrored the social inequities that women experienced. Thus changes in the structure of society demanded corresponding changes in language that had reinforced chauvinistic gender stereotypes. Not everybody has accepted these observations, but there is no doubt that educators, publishers, and the official language of media and the government are committed to the use of inclusive language.

Yet we make use of mostly masculine language in referring to God. Where does this leave people who have negative associations with their human fathers? The abuser and the alcoholic leave deep emotional scars on their children that often affect all their subsequent relationships. For many, painful experiences with their earthly fathers make it extremely difficult for them to relate to God as a loving, caring parent. For someone who has never experienced fatherly love, the phrase "heavenly Father" can be a stumbling block to prayer.

In that case, prayer may begin more profitably with "Lord Jesus" or "Holy Spirit" or "Loving God." I once asked members of a Bible study group which member of the Trinity they were most likely to address in prayer. They split about half and half between praying to God the Father and God the Son, while a smaller number prayed to God the Holy Spirit. Some Christians are very particular about employing the proper form of address in prayer, but I don't believe the Lord is too concerned about which person of the Trinity we pray to and through, as long as we pray. In God's great wisdom and mercy, we have been given differing ways of understanding and relating to God. If you pray to the Father, you might try expanding your prayer by cultivating awareness of the Spirit through addressing your prayer to the Holy Spirit. If you always pray to the Spirit, it would be good to add prayer to the Son and the Father, whom the Spirit is eager to glorify.

When we pray "our Father in heaven," we are saying that God is both like and different from an earthly father, since God is "in heaven." Some contemporary Christian crusaders, motivated by compassion for those who have had no positive experience of an earthly father, urge us to take seriously the analogical use of language and to promote multifaceted images for God.[8] The Bible is not without maternal images for God, for example, "As a mother comforts her child, so I will comfort you" (Is 66:13), and "Jerusalem, Jerusalem, the city that kills the prophets and stones those who are sent to it! How often have I desired to gather your children together as a hen gathers her brood under her wings, and you were not willing!" (Mt 23:37). Of course some people have had painful experiences with their mothers, and so this image can carry unwanted baggage too.

Some fortunate individuals have been able to differentiate their experiences with their earthly fathers from their understanding of God as heavenly Father. I recently spoke with a pastor's daughter who remembers her father as being quite judgmental and often absent, but nevertheless she knows God as an ever-present God of tender mercy. The experience of her father's example did not leave a judgmental imprint on her soul. It is not always true that our relationship with God is determined by our relationship with our father, but this should not lead us to minimize the personal testimony of those for whom addressing God as Father has been a significant hindrance.

Those who have a broken understanding of human parents have a special need to understand God's true character as a loving, caring and fair parent in their lives. Since Old Testament times, we have been told that a relationship with God heals the wounds of parental neglect and abandonment. As the prophet Hosea says, "In you the orphan finds mercy" (Hos 14:3). Those who have broken relationships with human parents find healing compassion in the God who is Father to the fatherless: "Father of orphans and protector of widows is God in his holy habitation. God gives the desolate a home to live in" (Ps 68:5-6). God has a special passion for orphans and widows and longs to see their psyches healed and their lives made whole. Undoubtedly this is why James writes, "Religion that is pure and undefiled before God, the Father, is this: to care for orphans and widows in their distress" (Jas 1:27).

I recently met Ellen Stamps, a disciple of Holocaust survivor Corrie ten Boom. Ellen was adopted as a child, but she always longed to know her birth parents. For much of her life, God seemed as absent as her unknown father and mother. She told me about a breakthrough she experienced while traveling with Corrie ten Boom through an airport in America. She heard an announcement over the loudspeakers that babies were arriving at gate 53. As an obstetrics nurse, she was eager to see these babies arrive; later she quipped, "I had seen babies come out a lot of ways, but never out of a plane!" She and Corrie went to the gate and saw nurses emerging from the plane, carrying Vietnamese babies and handing them to waiting adoptive parents.

Ellen was appalled to see one nurse handing a baby to the father instead of the mother. Her training and instincts had led her to believe that the bond with the mother was of primary importance. She was even more shocked to see the baby cling to the adoptive father and say as if on cue, "Papa!"

As she began to cry, God used the experience to heal a deep wound in her soul. For the first time she saw how it is possible to love a "papa" one has never seen and to be totally loved by a father who once seemed remote. For the first time in her prayers, she was able to call out to her loving heavenly Father. It is still true that in God "the orphan finds mercy." God is a loving parent to the parentless.

Questions for Further Reflection

1. Who do you think of when you pray?

2. Are you more likely to begin prayers with "Dear Father," "Lord Jesus" or "Holy Spirit"? Why?

3. In what ways has your relationship with your earthly parent(s) positively or adversely affected your relationship with God?

4. There are dozens of names for the Lord in the Bible that we can use to address God in prayer. Ponder this partial list and then explain which names are most meaningful for you.

Jesus

Wonderful Counselor (Is 9:6)

Mighty God (Is 9:6)

Prince of Peace (Is 9:6)

Holy One (Mk 1:24)

Son of the Most High (Lk 1:32)

Emmanuel, God with Us (Mt 1:23)

Lamb of God (Jn 1:29)

Author of Life (Acts 3:15)

Lord God the Almighty (Rev 15:3)

Lion of the Tribe of Judah (Rev 5:5)

Root of David (Rev 22:16)

Word of Life (1 Jn 1:1)

King of Kings (Rev 19:16)

"I am" (Jn 8:23)

Lord of Lords (Rev 19:16)

Advocate (1 Jn 2:1)

The Way, the Truth, the Life (Jn 14:6)

Dawn from on High (Lk 1:78)

Lord of All (Acts 10:36)

Messiah (Jn 1:41)

Son of God (Jn 1:34)

Savior (2 Pet 2:20)

Shepherd and Guardian of Your Souls (1 Pet 2:25)

Pioneer and Perfecter of Our Faith (Heb 12:2)

Cornerstone (Eph 2:20)

Righteous Judge (2 Tim 4:8)

Light of the World (Jn 8:12)

Morning Star (Rev 22:16)

Head over All Things for the Church (Eph 1:22)

Chief Shepherd (1 Pet 5:4)

Resurrection and Life (Jn 11:25)

Alpha and Omega (Rev 21:6)

5. Are you more likely to seek God's face or God's hand when you pray?

6. What are some specific ways you can pray for God's holy name to be honored in your life? your neighborhood? your church? your broader community? the nation and the world?

7. Why is "dear Father" a better understanding of *abba* than "daddy"?

8. Which is more emphasized in your relationship with God: intimacy or respect? obedience or mercy?

6

Seeking God's Rule in Prayer

Your kingdom come.
MATTHEW 6:10

As *the curtain lifts on the biblical drama, all creation is under* God's rule and authority. Adam and Eve are given considerable freedom, along with a test of their loyalty to God's kingdom: will they obey God or will they eat fruit from the forbidden "tree of the knowledge of good and evil" (Gen 2:17)? The suspense is short-lived, since God's idyllic kingdom lasts through only two chapters of the Genesis account. By chapter three, humankind has disobeyed God's rule, and the rest of the drama is the story of a rebellious humanity, a crumbling creation and the relentless mercy of a gracious God.

When we pray "your kingdom come," we are praying for the complete restoration of all humanity and all creation to God's rule and authority. We can never go back to Eden (Gen 3:22-24), but we can pray for a reestablishment of Eden's way of life—one creation under God. We begin by seeking God's face in prayer and asking, "Your kingdom come." As Jesus comments later in

Matthew 6, "But strive first for the kingdom of God and his righteousness, and all these things will be given to you as well" (Mt 6:33 par. Lk 12:31). To strive for God's kingdom is to join God in the reestablishment of divine sovereignty in our lives and throughout the universe. Unlike Eden, the kingdom of God "shall never be destroyed . . . and it shall stand forever" (Dan 2:44).

In some ways, it is easier to define what God's kingdom is not: war, famine, unforgiveness, cold-heartedness, selfishness, racism, nationalism, denominationalism, sin (of any sort). Wherever God rules, wherever a person or a group of people submit to God's direction, there the kingdom is. Praying for God's coming kingdom cannot be sharply differentiated from praying for God's holy name to be honored (petition one), nor from praying for God's will to be done (petition three). One of my college professors, Dale Bruner, taught me a memorable outline that uses *h* words to pray the four components of "your kingdom come": kingdom of the heart, kingdom of heaven, kingdom in history, kingdom in the homily.[1]

The Kingdom of the Heart

First, when we pray "your kingdom come," we are praying that God's reign will begin with us, in the core of our being. We pray that our personal lives will be restored to a full submission to the reign of God in Christ. The kingdom is in the first place personally experienced and validated: "For the kingdom of God is . . . righteousness and peace and joy in the Holy Spirit" (Rom 14:17).

To pray that the kingdom of God will come into our hearts is to recognize that the presence of Jesus is an invasion of the kingdom of God into this present rebellious age (Mt 12:28). When Jesus says "the kingdom of God is among you" (Lk 17:21), he refers to how he, as God's Son, mediates the presence of the kingdom. When we become Christians, Christ's indwelling presence provides us with a foretaste of the kingdom of God. "It is no longer I who live, but it is Christ who lives in me. And the life I now live in the flesh I live by faith in the Son of God, who loved me and gave himself for me" (Gal 2:20).

When we pray "Your kingdom come," we are praying, "Let it begin with me as I come to live under the lordship of Jesus in the power of the Spirit." The kingdom of God consists of loyal subjects who have sworn allegiance to it. "Your kingdom come" is first a swearing of our own allegiance to God's rule and purpose for all creation.

The Kingdom of Heaven

Second, when we pray for God's kingdom, we are asking for Jesus to come again as he promised. "Your kingdom come" is much like the Aramaic prayer of the early church, *Maranatha*, "Our Lord, come!" (1 Cor 16:22). Though we have a foretaste of God's coming kingdom through Christ who indwells us, we know that we have not yet seen the fullness of God's kingdom. Therefore, we are praying for an end to this present evil age and for the full presence of God's kingdom. "In accordance with his promise, we wait for new heavens and a new earth, where righteousness is at home" (2 Pet 3:13).

Why does Jesus teach us to pray for heaven to come? The experience of the early church demonstrates that it became difficult for Christians to maintain a fervent expectancy that Christ would return (1-2 Thess; 1-2 Pet). How much more difficult is it for us, living two thousand years later! Then and now, we are tempted to settle into a "this-is-it" mentality, losing a hunger for the complete wholeness that heaven will bring. Jesus needs to remind us to remember and to pray for "what no eye has seen, nor ear heard, nor the human heart conceived, what God has prepared for those who love him" (1 Cor 2:9).

Traditionally, the Advent season was a time to renew our prayers for the second coming of Christ. But somewhere along the way, the focus of Advent shifted back to Christ's first coming. We need to renew the older tradition so that at every Christmas season we readjust ourselves to the futurity of the kingdom, praying that God will soon bring the kingdom's fullness at the second coming of Christ, just as he brought the kingdom's first fruits at the first coming of Christ. "Your kingdom come" is a prayer for the end of the age that is echoed in the traditional ending of the Lord's Prayer, "For yours is the kingdom, and the power, and the glory, forever. Amen."[2] "Your kingdom come" is a call for the day when the loud voice from heaven will proclaim, "Now have come the salvation and the power and the kingdom of our God and the authority of his Messiah" (Rev 12:10). "The one who testifies to these things says, 'Surely I am coming soon' " (Rev 22:20). We are to respond to this promise of Jesus with our heartfelt prayer, "Amen. Come, Lord Jesus!" (Rev 22:20).

The Kingdom in History

Lewis Smedes once asked an ethics class I was taking, "How many of you want to go to heaven?" All hands went up. Then he asked, "How many want to go to heaven right now?" Many hands dropped. He followed up with "How many of you want all suffering to cease? All hunger to vanish? All war to end? All cancer to be healed? All sorrow to be vanquished?" All hands went up again. Then he said something I will never forget: "Then you all want to go to heaven right now." Prayer for the kingdom to come is prayer for justice to be done even and especially now.

Third, when we pray "your kingdom come," we are asking God to bring more of heaven's justice and peace to the current historical situation. Between the first and second comings of Christ, there is a gradual and growing realization of God's rule in the world. In this sense the kingdom is like a tiny mustard seed that grows until its impact is immense (Mk 4:31-32). The kingdom of God is not merely about a personal experience (heart) and a future expectancy (heaven). It also includes God's rule in the present—a tangible, historical reality. When Jesus cured the sick, he could say to them, "The kingdom of God has come near to you" (Lk 10:9). Reading Jesus' parables about the kingdom gives us a sense of the multifaceted way we experience God's rule both here and now, not merely "in the sweet bye and bye."

When we pray for God's kingdom to come, we are praying for peace and justice in real social and political terms. The heartfelt cry of the prophet Amos still echoes the heartbeat of God, "Let justice roll down like waters, and righteousness like an everflowing stream" (Amos 5:24). Where the kingdom of God is, there is justice (*dikaiosunē*, 2 Pet 3:13). Even though we do not see the fullness of the kingdom until God sovereignly closes this chapter of history, we are to live under God's rule in the here and now. Living under God's rule means that we hunger for the justice and the peace of the fullness of the kingdom.

The Kingdom in the Homily

Finally, we pray that the kingdom will come through its proclamation (the word *homily* means "sermon"). In Mark 1:15, Jesus tells his hearers that they experience the kingdom of God if they repent and believe the good message that he proclaims. In Mark 4, he uses the parable of the seed and the sower to describe how the kingdom of God is spread through the teaching and the proclamation of the word about Jesus. When we pray for God's kingdom to come, we are praying for those who sow the seed of God's word and for those who harvest souls and enfold them in the church.

When we pray for preachers and teachers of God's Word, we are praying for their kingdom-bearing role. In a very compelling description of the importance of those who proclaim God's Word, Paul writes:

> But how are they to call on one in whom they have not believed? And how are they to believe in one of whom they have never heard? And how are they to hear without someone to proclaim him? And how are they to proclaim him unless they are sent? As it is written, "How beautiful are the feet of those who bring good news!" But not all have obeyed the good news; for Isaiah says, "Lord, who has believed our message?" So faith comes from what is heard, and what is heard comes through the word of Christ. (Rom 10:14-17)

Thus prayers for missionaries, preachers, and Bible teachers are prayers that God's kingdom will come through the preaching and teaching of the Word. It is through powerful proclamation of the cross of Christ that the kingdom of God is spread abroad.

When we pray for God's kingdom to come, we pray for the personal dimension of this petition: Rule over me! We pray for the future fulfillment of the ancient promises: Reign in fullness! We pray for the present realization of the coming kingdom: Rule out injustice and bring wholeness to every brokenness! We pray for the bearers of the message about the God of love who has come to us in Jesus Christ our Lord: Rule over all through the spread of your Word!

Questions for Reflection

1. Do you pray for Christ to come again? Why or why not?

2. Where is there an absence of God's kingdom in your community? How can you participate in "seeking first God's kingdom and his justice" for that community need?

3. Is there any aspect of your life that you need to subject to God's rule? What changes will you need to make as you let God take charge of that part of your life?

4. Which of the four dimensions of the kingdom of God do you usually think of when you pray, "Your kingdom come"?

5. Which of these four do you seldom think of?

6. Do you have a list of Christian workers for whom you pray? If not, consider making a list and posting it where it will remind you to pray for them. (One person I know covers her refrigerator with pictures of the Christian workers for whom she prays.)

7

Seeking God's Will in Prayer

Your will be done.
MATTHEW 6:10

Jesus lived fully under God's rule and authority. "My food," he said, "is to do the will of him who sent me and to complete his work" (Jn 4:34). Jesus' life was driven by a single purpose—doing God's bidding: "I can do nothing on my own. As I hear, I judge; and my judgment is just, because I seek to do not my own will but the will of him who sent me" (Jn 5:30). Jesus submitted to God's authority, and he taught us to pray, "Your will be done." This is why biblical theologian Oscar Cullmann says, "One of the main characteristics of New Testament prayer is union with God's will."[1] Jesus models for us the essence of both the Christian life and the life of prayer: being yielded to God's gracious and sovereign purpose.

When we pray for God's will to be done, we further refine our request for the kingdom to come in fullness. We will consider this topic in terms of (1) praying for a yielded will, (2) praying for an understanding of God's Word and the ability to do it and

(3) praying for an awareness of God's direction.

A Prayer to Yield to God's Will

When we pray "your will be done," we align ourselves with Jesus in submission to God's will. We reaffirm our Christian confession—Jesus is Lord—by reasserting our willingness to go his way and to do his bidding. This is the essential first step to understanding God's will.

What we need to learn first about God's will is not *what* we should do. There is no point in knowing what God wants us to do if we are not committed to doing what God wants to be done. Doing God's will is first about having the "want to." When we have the "want to," then the "what to" readily reveals itself. Getting the "want to" is not easy. Longing for God's will involves breaking down our willfulness, much as a horse needs to be broken to become useful.

Jesus was so yielded that "he humbled himself and became obedient to the point of death—even death on a cross" (Phil 2:8). We should not suppose that crucifixion was easy for him to face. Just before his arrest in the garden of Gethsemane, he wrestled with God in prayer, pleading with God to allow another outcome. But Jesus' yielded will is evident as he pleads and pours out his fully human emotions: "My Father, if it is possible, let this cup pass from me; yet not what I want but what you want" (Mt 26:39). Jesus is obviously experiencing severe conflict. He cries out to God a second and a third time, begging for an alternative to the cross, but each time he yields to God's purpose—"your will be done" (vv. 42-44).

When we hear Jesus praying these four words of the Lord's Prayer in the garden of Gethsemane, "your will be done," we are confronted with what this petition can mean for us. If Jesus' yielding resulted in the cross, then our yielding could lead to equally challenging consequences. The apostle Paul, for example, found that suffering accompanied his submission to God's will: "I want to know Christ and the power of his resurrection *and the sharing of his sufferings by becoming like him in his death*" (Phil 3:10, emphasis added). When we pray "your will be done," we are praying sobering words indeed!

Charles Spurgeon was a great nineteenth-century preacher, and much of his preaching about prayer involves explaining what God must do in us for us to know and do God's will. Spurgeon says, "Is it not a curious thing that, whenever God means to make a man great, He always breaks him in pieces first?"[2] This is the example provided by Jesus and his followers, and is echoed in the witness of the spiritual giants who have walked the face of the earth. To yield to God's purposes, our will must be broken and tamed:

> Have none of you ever noticed, in your own lives, that whenever God is going to give you an enlargement, and bring you out to a larger sphere of service, or a higher platform of spiritual life, you always get thrown down? That is His usual way of working; He makes you hungry before He feeds you; He strips you before He robes you; He makes nothing of you before He makes something of you. This was the way with David. He is to be king in Jerusalem; but he must go to the throne by the way of the cave. Now, are any of you here going to heaven, or going to a more heavenly state of sanctification, or going to a greater sphere of usefulness: Do not wonder if you go by the way of the cave.[3]

When we know the depth of our need for God and when we are convinced that God's purpose is far superior to our preference, then we are ready to yield to God and to do God's will. "Your will be done" is a prayer that God will bridle us and direct us, wherever that may lead.

Remarkably, "confidence teaching" asserts that we should not pray "your will be done" because praying this constitutes an admission that we are not sure of what we are asking for. That is, praying "your will be done" is said to be an expression of doubt that God will answer our prayer. Confidence teaching asserts that God answers bold claims, not the faltering prayers that tack on the opt-out clause "yet not what I ask but what you want." Here is one example of this approach:

> Many wonderful prayers have gone unanswered because they were rendered powerless with the word "if" in the middle of them. Why do people do this? [John] Bisagno suggests that the real reason behind this is: "We do not really believe that God is going to do anything so we have an easy way out in case He doesn't—an escape clause in fine print." In other words, many people do not have biblical faith. [4]

Such confidence teaching, while encouraging us to be bold in praying for the miraculous and the impossible, implicitly criticizes Jesus himself as he prayed in Gethsemane (Mt 26:39), and it goes directly against his instruction in the Lord's Prayer. The point is this: we do not order God around when we pray. Rather, when we pray for God's will we realign our purpose and direction to whatever purpose and direction God chooses for us.

Since the 1750s, Methodists have prayed a yielding prayer at the first service of the year. John Wesley, an eighteenth-century Anglican reformer, encouraged them to take seriously the lordship of Christ and Jesus' prayer of yielding. Wesley's Covenant Prayer is a detailed expansion of "your will be done":

> Leader Prays: Lord God, Holy Father, since you have called us through Christ to share in this gracious Covenant, we take upon ourselves with joy the yoke of obedience, and, for love of you, engage ourselves to seek and do your perfect will. We are no longer our own, but yours.
>
> All Pray: I am no longer my own, but yours. Put me to what you will, rank me with whom you will; put me to doing, put me to suffering; let me be employed for you or laid aside for you, exalted

for you or brought low for you; let me be full, let me be empty; let me have all things, let me have nothing; I freely and wholeheartedly yield all things to your pleasure and disposal. And now, glorious and blessed God, Father, Son, and Holy Spirit, you are mine and I am yours. So be it. And the covenant now made on earth, let it be ratified in heaven. Amen.[5]

If we find this severe, then we have fully grasped the radical nature of praying "your will be done." The first several times I prayed this prayer, its implications did not really sink in. But as I have come to take more and more seriously the yielded life, this prayer and "your will be done" have taken on more and more depth. Perhaps that is why it is good to pray the Lord's Prayer often. The first repetitions are like raindrops hitting dry ground. But as we pray it continuously, the ground of our spirit is softened, and we are able to more fully receive the refreshing and nourishing rain of God's presence and will in our lives.

A Prayer to Do God's Word

Have you ever presented a request to someone who responded, "Let me pray about it"? In many situations this is an appropriate response, showing that this person is and wants to be yielded to God's purpose and direction. I would never accept a job or move my family or take on a major commitment without first seeking God's guidance and permission in prayer.

But some situations require an immediate response. If your neighbor is bleeding and needs immediate assistance, pausing to pray is a heartless and godless thing to do. We already know God's will for this circumstance—love your neighbor as you love yourself. James puts it this way: "If a brother or sister is naked and lacks daily food, and one of you says to them, 'Go in peace; keep warm and eat your fill,' and yet you do not supply their bodily needs, what is the good of that?" (Jas 2:15-16). Likewise, if a person comes to us with a need we can meet and if our response is only "Let me pray about it," then our faith is dead and we merely use spiritual-sounding language to hide our lack of knowledge of God and God's will for us.

God has revealed much of the divine will in Scripture. We need not pray about whether or not to commit adultery because God has already revealed that adultery is wrong (Ex 20:14). We are wrong to ask God if we should go to worship this week because God has already revealed that we should not neglect our regular gathering together (Heb 10:25). If someone asks us to enter into an illegal partnership, we take God's name in vain if we respond, "Let me ask God about it." God wants us to answer no, as God has already told us clearly in Scripture. When we ask for God's desire to be done, we pray that God will cause us to know and understand the divine will revealed in Scripture. As we study God's commands, we learn God's expectations regarding such matters as worship, relationships, use of money and time. Understanding God's Word sets us in the direction God has revealed we are all to head.

Doing God's will goes beyond knowing God's will. Our prayer is that we will act on the knowledge we acquire, "Your will be *done*." It is necessary to pray for the doing of God's will because obeying God is not a natural inclination of fallen humanity. Like the apostle Paul, "I do not understand my own actions. For I do not do what I want, but I do the very thing I hate. . . . For I delight in the law of God in my inmost self, but I see in my members another law at war with the law of my mind, making me captive to the law of sin that dwells in my members" (Rom 7:15-23). Knowing what God wants is not enough. We need God's help to do all that we have been taught.

When we pray this petition of the Lord's Prayer, it helps to keep its immediate context in mind. The setting for the Lord's Prayer in Matthew is the Sermon on the Mount. These chapters,

Matthew 5—7, contain Jesus' most strenuous teaching on many subjects:

> Blessed are those who are persecuted for righteousness' sake. (5:10)

> Unless your righteousness exceeds that of the scribes and Pharisees, you will never enter the kingdom of heaven. (5:20)

> You have heard that it was said to those of ancient times, "You shall not murder"; and "whoever murders shall be liable to judgment." But I say to you that if you are angry with a brother or sister, you will be liable to judgment. (5:21-22)

> I say to you that everyone who looks at a woman with lust has already committed adultery with her in his heart. (5:28)

> If your right hand causes you to sin, cut it off and throw it away; it is better for you to lose one of your members than for your whole body to go into hell. (5:30)

> If anyone strikes you on the right cheek, turn the other also; and if anyone wants to sue you and take your coat, give your cloak as well; and if anyone forces you to go one mile, go also the second mile. (5:39-41)

> Love your enemies and pray for those who persecute you. (5:44)

If we are honest, we will admit that these commands are difficult to obey. When we pray "your will be done," we are praying that God will enable us to obey these demanding commands. We ask that God will establish our house on the rock of God's will: "Everyone then who hears these words of mine and acts on them will be like a wise man who built his house on rock. The rain fell, the floods came, and the winds blew and beat on that house, but it did not fall, because it had been founded on rock" (Mt 7:24-25).

When we pray for God's will to be done, we yield to God's

purpose and seek God's strength to obey God's Word. Even so, in our daily lives there are times when we need divine guidance in our decision-making. We pray "your will be done" seeking to be directed by God's Spirit.

A Prayer for God to Direct Us

Recently a friend of mine came to a crossroads in his career. Fortunately he had several job offers. Unfortunately he could not decide which one to accept. In his confusion he quipped, "I wouldn't know the will of God if it walked by in a Hawaiian shirt." As he wrestled with his options, he prayed fervently, "Your will be done." An answer took time to emerge, and my friend found great comfort in the embrace of God's love.

It is important for us to seek God's guidance because, as someone has said, "Our greatest enemy is not the obvious evil but the apparent good." Satan goes about masquerading as an angel of light, not a scary demon (2 Cor 11:14). How then should we seek God's directive will regarding important decisions that we face? There are several pointers that you may find helpful.

1. Begin and end significant decision-making with prayer. Jesus prayed intensely before big decisions, such as selecting his disciples. My wife and I once decided to buy a house without praying about it. A year and a half later we were led to move, and, in a depressed California housing market, the house became a millstone around our necks. It took us four years to extract ourselves from that situation. One thing is clear: we did not pray before deciding to buy, and we lived to regret our decision. It was the worst misstep in our fifteen-year marriage.

2. Prayerful decision-making is not to be set against our powers of reasoning and what we have learned from experience. Paul says to be transformed by the "renewal" of our minds, not the "removal" of our minds (Rom 12:1-2). The guidance of the Holy Spirit may transcend what we think, but not necessarily in every case or even in most cases.

3. Prayerful decision-making has clear boundaries marked out by Scripture. When we pray for direction, we should refresh ourselves with the counsel of God. "Your word is a lamp to my feet and a light to my path" (Ps 119:105). Is there something that we can learn from Abraham or Sarah, Ruth or David, Moses or Jesus, Peter or Paul that might help us in our situation? Much of God's directive is already revealed in the Scriptures.

4. Prayerful decision-making involves consulting the body of Christ. The church is God's gift to us, and the thoughtful advice of caring friends can make a big difference in our perspective on any particular problem or situation. As we consult God in prayer and in the Word, it is equally important that we rely on the gifts of wisdom and knowledge that God has distributed in the body of Christ around us (see 1 Cor 12).

5. Prayerful decision-making may embolden us, or it may caution us. Sometimes God needs to cheer us on to do something that we might not do without that special incentive from the Holy Spirit. Or we may be headed down the wrong path, and the Holy Spirit checks us and slows down our mad rush toward a bad thing. Recently my wife and I prayed about an important financial decision. We were eager to make a certain investment, but when we prayed we received no clear guidance other than a shared sense that God wanted us to wait on making the decision. Four months later we realized that God had given us perfect guidance, and we rejoiced that we had not proceeded on our own. Even though our heads said go, God's guidance to proceed slowly was really saying no.

6. Prayerful decision-making does not rule out personal responsibility. The act of praying about something does not relieve us of our accountability for the results of our decision. Prayer is not an insurance policy that covers losses resulting from foolish decision making. Jesus prayed before he announced that Peter and Judas would be his disciples. At times Peter seemed to be anything but a promising leader, and Judas's betrayal, at the moment, may have appeared to suggest that both Jesus' praying and his decision-making were flawed. In hindsight, though, we see that both Peter and Judas were essential to the fulfillment of God's purpose in Christ.

7. *Sometimes heaven is silent.* Sometimes God does not appear to have an opinion on the subject. Then we "pay our pennies and take our choices." Sometimes we have to make the best decision we can, confident that our God of grace will cause the good and merciful divine purpose to work through our finite human plans. When the heavens are silent and God does not answer our prayers, we still trust God to be in control. "We know that all things work together for good for those who love God, who are called according to his purpose" (Rom 8:28).[6] In words of an inspired bumper sticker, "The will of God will never lead you where the grace of God cannot keep you."

On Earth As It Is in Heaven

When we finish praying "your will be done," Jesus adds, "on earth as it is in heaven." At this point we find ourselves exactly half way through the Lord's Prayer. We have now asked God to hallow his name, to bring his kingdom and to impose his will, as in heaven. We end the first half of the Lord's Prayer by asking that we may see these aspects of God's will fulfilled on earth as the angels see them fulfilled in heaven.

Earlier we prayed "may your holy name be honored." Now we expand that with "on earth as it is in heaven." Isaiah 6 gives us one picture of how God's name is hallowed in heaven. The heavenly beings fly above God on the throne, and they shout to one another, "Holy, holy, holy is the LORD of hosts; the whole earth is full of his glory" (Is 6:3). As Isaiah witnesses this vision, he realizes that he is not worthy to speak God's precious name. Then one of the seraphs flies to him and touches his mouth with a burning coal, symbolizing Isaiah's purification. After that he can speak God's name and address God in the throne room of heaven. Thus we pray that our earthly experience will mirror heaven's model of how God's name is honored, how God's rule is complete, and how God's will is perfectly done.

"On earth as it is in heaven" is a turning point in the prayer in two ways: (1) it applies to the preceding three petitions and (2) it shifts its focus from God in heaven to needs and struggles that we face on earth. The first three petitions are about God's name, God's kingdom and God's will. The last three petitions are about our sustenance, our forgiveness and our deliverance.

In heaven
1. Hallow your name
2. Bring your kingdom
3. Impose your will

On earth
4. Give us bread
5. Forgive us as we forgive
6. Deliver us

Throughout we ask that God will cause our experience on earth to reflect the model of heaven. We are praying that our present experience will come to completely reflect God's heavenly reality "on earth as it is in heaven."

Questions for Further Reflection

1. To what extent have you surrendered your life and your will to God?

2. What evidence can you produce from your calendar and

your checkbook that God's will prevails in your life?

3. Have you gone through a season or seasons of breaking? What was the result spiritually?

4. Can you pray Wesley's Covenant Prayer with your whole heart? What lines or phrases, if any, cause you to hesitate? Why?

I am no longer my own, but yours. Put me to what you will, rank me with whom you will; put me to doing, put me to suffering; let me be employed for you or laid aside for you, exalted for you or brought low for you; let me be full, let me be empty; let me have all things, let me have nothing; I freely and wholeheartedly yield all things to your pleasure and disposal. And now, glorious and blessed God, Father, Son, and Holy Spirit, you are mine and I am yours. So be it. And the covenant now made on earth, let it be ratified in heaven. Amen.

5. Are you aware of any aspect of your life that is not in conformity with God's will as you know it from Scripture? What changes do you need to make to cause your life to reflect your prayer that God's will be done?

6. Faithful Bible study focuses both on content and on character. How often do you read and study the Bible to learn more of what it says? Do you end your reading and study time by applying what you have read to how you choose to live?

7. What commands of God do you find hardest to obey? Consider spending time praying for God's strength to obey these commands too.

8. Do you consider prayer, Bible study and consultation with other Christians when you make significant decisions? Why or why not? What are the dangers of "too spiritual" an approach to decisions? What are the dangers of "too rational" an approach?

9. What aspects of your life would be different if you were now

living in heaven before the throne of God instead of on earth? Make those differences a matter of prayer as you pray for God's name to be honored, God's kingdom to come, and God's will to be done "on earth as it is in heaven."

8

Seeking God's Hand in Prayer

Give us this day our daily bread.
MATTHEW 6:11

The first half of the Lord's Prayer mirrors Jesus' teaching that we should strive first for God, God's kingdom and God's righteousness. The second half of the prayer turns to our human experience, beginning with a request for God to meet our basic needs, such as "daily bread." After we have sought God's face and God's purposes in the first half of the prayer, we are ready to ask for our needs and concerns—to seek God's hand in prayer. The focus on God's concerns in the first half of the prayer now expands to address our interests.

The context for the Lord's Prayer makes a connection between approaching God as "our Father in heaven" and the request for daily bread. Prayer begins with a relationship with God that calls us to a trusting reliance on God for our life needs. Following the Lord's Prayer (in both Matthew and Luke), Jesus urges us to trust God to meet our needs just as children intuitively trust their parents:

> Ask, and it will be given you; search, and you will find; knock, and the door will be opened for you. For everyone who asks receives, and everyone who searches finds, and for everyone who knocks, the door will be opened. Is there anyone among you who, if your child asks for bread, will give a stone? Or if the child asks for a fish, will give a snake? If you then, who are evil, know how to give good gifts to your children, how much more will your Father in heaven give good things to those who ask him! (Mt 7:7-11 par. Lk 11:9-13)

Jesus reminds us of God's good intention for us. We should not expect God to care less than our parents about the needs we have. The One who sees every sparrow fall to the ground and has numbered every hair on our heads frets over the real needs we have for food, water and clothing.

Praying for What We Need

For those who speak English, asking for "daily bread" is a straightforward concept: we ask God for what we need today. But many scholars have suggested other nuances for the rare Greek adjective used here, *epiousios*, which we translate "daily." Strikingly, this is the only adjective used in the entire prayer. Perhaps Jesus meant that we should think of our daily life as being like that of the Israelites as they wandered in the desert after their deliverance from Egypt. As God provided manna for them each day, so we trust God to meet our daily need for food. Or perhaps Jesus meant for us to ask God to provide spiritual nourishment, "true bread" through God's Word and through the bread of the sacrament of the Lord's Supper.[1] A passage in John's Gospel makes this approach to "daily bread" plausible:

> So they said to him, "What sign are you going to give us then, so that we may see it and believe you? What work are you performing? Our ancestors ate the manna in the wilderness; as it is written, 'He gave them bread from heaven to eat.' " Then Jesus said to them, "Very truly, I tell you, it was not Moses who gave you the bread from heaven, but it is my Father who gives you the true bread from heaven. For

the bread of God is that which comes down from heaven and gives life to the world." They said to him, "Sir, give us this bread always." Jesus said to them, "I am the bread of life. Whoever comes to me will never be hungry, and whoever believes in me will never be thirsty." (Jn 6:30-35)

Some scholars take *epiousios* to refer to "the *next* day's bread." They take the "next day" to be the next age when God's kingdom has come in fullness. In other words, they propose that Jesus is teaching us to pray for the nourishment of his coming kingdom—the "next day" in spiritual history waiting to unfold. But this suggested meaning is improbable,[2] and such spiritual interpretations of "daily bread" make a rare adjective bear too much theological weight.

In 1925 a scrap of paper was discovered. On it was written a household account listing everyday provisions.[3] The word *epiousios*, "daily," appears in this list. This usage of the word suggests that Jesus probably did not have some hidden or lofty intention here. His words mean simply "Pray for the essentials you need today." He goes on to say as much in the Sermon on the Mount, calling us to substitute prayer for worry in regard to our daily provisions:

> Do not worry, saying, "What will we eat?" or "What will we drink?" or "What will we wear?" . . . Indeed your heavenly Father knows that you need all these things. But strive first for the kingdom of God and his righteousness, and all these things will be given to you as well. (Mt 6:31-33)

Thus "give us today our daily bread" is a request to our loving heavenly Father to provide for our ordinary earthly needs.

The difference between a need and a want has become muddled in our language because the distinction is muddled in our materialistic society. When Unabomber suspect Theodore J. Kaczynski was captured in Montana, news reports went into minute detail regarding his eccentric life. My wife, trying to explain the meaning of the word *eccentric* to a group of adults learning English as a second language, explained that Kaczynski chose to live in a small one-room cabin without electricity or running water. But this explanation did not work for a student from Pakistan, who said, "I don't understand. That is how most of the people in my country live." What is eccentric to Westerners may be normal life to others!

What basic needs are referred to here? Jesus lists food, water and clothing when he urges us not to worry about what we need (Mt 6:31-32). The apostle Paul experienced a stark life as a missionary; nevertheless, he had learned to be content in all circumstances (Phil 4:11-13). He instructs his disciple Timothy on the distinction between a need and a want, reminding us that "we brought nothing into the world, so that we can take nothing out of it; but if we have food and clothing, we will be content with these" (1 Tim 6:7-8). This does not mean that we should not pray about other basic needs such as shelter, meaningful work, loving relationships, inner peace and the like. Rather, it reminds us to be grateful for the "simple bare necessities," in the words of a favorite children's song.

"Give us bread" keeps us from coming to see prayer as a vending machine where we drop in a prayer and out comes our Christmas wish list. Asking for essentials (and thus reminding ourselves of their importance) helps us avoid a "gimme" attitude, a "spirituality of me." When we pray for basic nourishment, we are countering the bombardment of advertisements designed to confuse needs and wants in our minds. We have already yielded up self-satisfaction when we pray "your will be done." Now we demonstrate our trust that God knows exactly what we need for a fulfilled life. We keep our requests basic because God has already promised that there is much more in store for those who anticipate the coming kingdom.

Although Jesus encourages us to ask for the basics, contemporary Americans tend not to. In a recent study, Margaret Poloma and George Gallup Jr. discovered that even though 88 percent of Americans pray to God in some way or other, only 42 percent of them ask for material things they might need. And only 15 percent report regularly receiving answers to specific prayer requests.[4] Perhaps many have forgotten that all seed comes from God. We can improve growth with fertilizer, but we cannot manufacture seed. Creation is radically dependent on God. *Radical* is the right word because it means "to cut to the root." To the roots, where the seed is—that is how dependent we are on God. Praying for bread is a reminder of our dependence on God, encouraging us not to take for granted seed and grain and flour and bread. God richly provides, and we humbly ask.

There is great practical wisdom in focusing our request on the coming day. "Give us what we need today" is very helpful prayer advice for those facing serious illness. Someone whose cancer has spread and whose time is short may find it difficult to know how to pray. Prayers for healing and relief come more easily in the early stages of disease than in the late stages, when the pain is intense. Despair lurks about those later stages, and the sufferer typically desires for life to end. Jesus' prayer helps us center on the present, "give us today what we need." As we stand at the base of a mountain looking up, our spirits may become anxious at the prospect of the long, steep ascent ahead. By focusing narrowly on each step, the needs of the day, we can make it to the top eventually. In the words of the old adage, "How do you eat an elephant? One bite at a time." We are encouraged to focus our prayers on the next bite.

Praying "Our" Daily Bread for a Hungry World

Do you ask for the bread you need today? Many of us live with overstuffed refrigerators and bodies. It is estimated that 20-30 percent of Americans are obese. Our inclination is to pray "help me eat less food" rather than "give me more." Within a stone's throw of our homes most of us have several grocery stores with enough food to feed entire villages plagued by famine. Isn't it heartless for us to ask for *more* food when there are so many on our planet who desperately need *some*?

But Jesus teaches us to pray for *us*, not *me*. The plural pronouns *us* and *our* expand these requests to include all those who live under the one Father in heaven. Prayer has a conscience. It is "give us," not "give me." Wealthy Christians in an age of hunger can passionately pray this petition for the hungry. With us the hungry claim, "Our Father in heaven." With them we plead, "Give those of us who need it basic bread." This prayer helps us call into question our overconsumption. Are we truly living under God's rule? When we pray for food for our brothers and sisters, is there simplicity and frugality in our lives consistent with the prayer we offer? Many of us might find John Wesley's choice too extreme. One of the wealthiest men in eighteenth-century England, he undertook a vegetarian lifestyle while he was at Oxford in view of the paralyzing poverty of the underclass of his day. His reason is as compelling now as it was then: "How can I eat meat when others have no bread?" He determined to live as simply as he could and earn as much as he could so that he could give alms for those living in hunger, squalor and poverty.

Praying for food for our hungry world is an aspect of praying for God's kingdom to come. We are all too well aware that much of the problem with world hunger is distribution, not supply. While countries such as the United States pay farmers not to grow food, thousands die of malnutrition every day. Even though there is an abundance of grains and other foods that can be airlifted to needy countries, the politics of those areas often thwart the distribution of food to those who need it. For example, during a famine in Ethiopia (1984-85), the Ethiopian government at first denied that there was a famine. When the government finally reached out for help, it seized and held shipments of food intended for the northern part of the country because the government was trying to quash a separatist movement there. Tons of food were stolen and sold by government officials, and much of the rest spoiled before it could reach starving populations.[5] Given our world situation, we pray "give *us* bread" at the same time we plead for God's kingdom to replace the corrupt governments that keep the seed that God has already provided from reaching those who desperately need it.

No one in the human family can really say, "I have nothing I need to pray for." There are virtually endless needs in our global village that we can remind God of in prayer. We pray for the great needs of hurting humanity when we pray, "Give *us* this day our daily bread." Furthermore, there is deep joy and abiding peace in learning how much we lean on God. Yes, we should "act as though it all depends on us," but we must learn to pray more and more "as though it all depends on God"—because it does.

Questions for Further Reflection

1. What, if anything, are you inclined to worry about? How can you substitute prayer for worry?

2. Have you ever prayed as you glanced through the newspaper? Try it, using the headlines, photographs and articles as your "prayer list."

3. Are you more likely to pray "I" or "we"? How does praying we, our and us keep our prayers from being selfish?

4. What needs do you know of right now for yourself or someone else? Take some time to make that person's "daily bread" a matter of focused prayer.

5. How is praying for God's kingdom wrapped up with praying "give us bread?"

6. What do you think about the assertion that food shortages are a problem of distribution, not supply?

7. Make a list of the items that you purchased last month that were needs and the ones that were wants. What could you eliminate from either list to be able to give more alms for the poor?

8. What, if anything, bothers you about the subject discussed in this chapter? Why?

9

Finding Forgiveness in Prayer

And forgive us our debts, as we also have forgiven
our debtors. . . . For if you forgive others their trespasses,
your heavenly Father will also forgive you;
but if you do not forgive others, neither will your
Father forgive your trespasses.
MATTHEW 6:12, 14-15

Whenever you stand praying, forgive, if you have anything
against anyone; so that your Father in heaven
may also forgive you your trespasses.
MARK 11:25

The movie War of the Roses *was based on a bitter marital breakup* involving a vindictive husband and a spiteful wife in Switzerland several years ago. He canceled one too many holidays, so she poured bicarbonate of soda into his rare tropical fish tank. He retaliated by putting her diamond jewelry down the garbage disposal. She got even by throwing his stereo equipment into the swimming pool. He lashed out by pouring liquid bleach on her $200,000 wardrobe. She struck back and poured house paint on his Ferrari. His reply was to kick a hole in her $180,000 painting by Picasso. Not finished, she opened the seacocks and sank his thirty-eight-foot yacht. Neither spouse had any legal recourse, since it was their property to do with as they liked. Fortunately, their family lawyer finally arranged an armistice between the feuding spouses. Retaliation solves nothing.

As all of us know, living with other humans is hurtful, bothersome and annoying. As long as we are alive, evil people will prowl and assault. Ironically, however, those who most often wrong us are usually the most precious people in our lives: spouses, parents, kids, bosses, coworkers, neighbors, friends, in-laws, church members. Sometimes they mean to injure us, but mostly they do it unintentionally and accidentally. It is not only what they do but also what they say and the hard looks they give us. Sometimes we take offense because we have wrongly interpreted their remarks. Living a life that is free of pain is not possible if we plan on living around other human beings.

How do we cope with the hurt and the annoyance that come our way? Ignoring hurt doesn't work. "Time heals all wounds" is bunk. Emotional wounds can fester and irritate for many years. For example, many divorced people know that divorce does not necessarily resolve the problems associated with an unhappy marriage. Ten years after divorce 41 percent of women and 31 percent of men still feel angry and rejected. People summon up great energy when they describe how someone hurt them several years before. We all know people who have moved, quit jobs, grown hedges or changed churches because of a real or an imagined injury they received from someone else. None of these responses to pain can actually free us from the pain of hurt—only forgiveness can do that. Unforgiveness also creates a barrier to effective prayer: Jesus says God does not want to talk to us if we are not talking to one of our brothers or sisters.

Forgiven If Forgiving

Forgiveness is the key for living with fallible friends and petty people, and it is the essential ingredient of an effective prayer life. Forgiveness is love's insurance policy. The gift of forgiveness enables us to live with flawed people. The most important thing we need to hear from this fifth petition of the Lord's Prayer is that receiving forgiveness from God is directly dependent on our willingness to offer forgiveness to others. Jesus says, "But if you do not forgive others, *neither will your Father forgive you.*" This is not some sort of works righteousness. It is the unmistakable word of Jesus. According to him, unforgiveness is a clear indication that there is trouble in our relationship with God, and any appeals we make to be forgiven by God are muffled by mercilessness on our part. This punch line immediately following the Lord's Prayer focuses us on the necessity of forgiving others. Of all the things that Jesus could have emphasized after teaching us this prayer, he dwells on the necessity of showing mercy to others if we are to receive God's mercy. We dare not minimize what the Master has emphasized.

In Matthew 18 Jesus tells a parable to demonstrate why we should offer others the same unconditional forgiveness God grants to us. Peter had obviously figured out how important forgiveness was to Jesus, so he asked a question, "How often should I forgive? As many as seven times?" Jesus then corrected him for trying to put any limits on grace and mercy: "Not seven times, but, I tell you, seventy-seven times" (Mt 18:21-22).[1] Jesus goes on to explain how forgiveness works under God's rule and authority. A king (who stands for God) forgave one of his slaves (symbolizing sinners like me and you) for a debt larger than he could ever pay in his lifetime. But that same slave turned around and refused to forgive a fellow slave the lunch money he had borrowed, demanding every nickel and dime. When the king found out, he "summoned him and said to him, 'You wicked slave! I forgave you all that debt because you pleaded with me. Should you not have had mercy on your fellow slave, as I had mercy on you?' And in anger his lord handed him over to be tortured until he would pay his entire debt." Jesus drives the point home for us with this ominous warning, "So my heavenly

Father will also do to every one of you, if you do not forgive your brother or sister from your heart" (Mt 18:32-35).

According to Jesus, forgiving others is not an option for Christians. We cannot rationalize away unforgiveness and harbor bitterness under the guise of a "personality conflict." In fact, he appears to make our salvation dependent on our willingness to pass on the mercy we receive from God. This is the Golden Rule with a twist: as we forgive others, so God forgives us. Failure to forgive others results in suspension of the pardon we have received for our sins. We receive forgiveness for our sins, provided we pass on that same mercy to others.

This is not to say that all forgiveness is easy. A small offense is easily dismissed, but a huge hurt or a repeated wrong is a different matter. Jesus' words to Peter can help us. Someone who wrongs us once needs to be forgiven once, while someone who repeatedly wrongs us requires multiplied forgiveness on our part.

A "thirty-day prayer covenant" has helped me in my struggles to forgive. I commit myself to asking God every day for thirty days to help me forgive someone. I pray for that person's well-being and ask God to help me love, following Jesus' instructions, "Bless those who curse you, pray for those who abuse you" (Lk 6:28 par. Mt 5:44). I seldom have had to pray the full thirty days before finding forgiveness and a new attitude toward that person. Sometimes forgiveness comes easily, while other times it is a healing process that takes time.[2]

Forgiving Others Frees Me

The story is told of a real estate developer who purchased downtown property to erect a high-rise and a parking lot. He successfully purchased everything he needed except one strip of land, which was a couple of yards wide and one hundred feet long. The owner of the land built a sliver of a house the length of his property to spite the developer. He lived in Spite House, as it was called, for many years before he died and his heir sold the property. He may have been completely justified in his anger at changes in the neighborhood he had lived in for so many years, but he is the one who "cut off his nose to spite his face." He had to live cramped and harassed in Spite House to keep the wrecking balls away. His vindictiveness hurt him more than anybody else.

Obeying Jesus' commandment to forgive enables us to enjoy the benefits of pulling bitter roots out of our lives. The hurt was bad enough, but harboring bitterness continues to diminish us. It is to our advantage to obey Christ, since forgiving others frees us. Bitterness is a poison that affects the one harboring it more severely than the object of the anger. My unforgiveness is a cold prison cell, lined with hurt and locked by condemnation.

One of Abraham Lincoln's biggest challenges was to lead the country in such a way that, if and when the North won the Civil War, there would still be a foundation standing on which a united nation could eventually be rebuilt. Once when he was stumping on the importance of mercy and forgiveness to fellow Americans, a man bitter over the loss of many family members addressed the president. "Where I come from we destroy our enemies," he said with venom. Lincoln wisely replied, "Do we not destroy our enemies when we make them our friends?" Forgiveness frees us as much as it frees our enemies.

Perhaps you have had this thought: *I can't forgive them for what they did.* You know that you were right and the other person was wrong. Your anger is justified. This is precisely what forgiveness is about—laying down our right to remain angry and giving up our claim to future repayment of the debt we have suffered. We are to be gracious toward those who wrong us because the amount we let go can never compare with the pardon God offers us through Christ. In fact, God's complete pardon of our every sin sets the absolute standard for how we should forgive each wrong done to us. He expects us to pass on the mercy we have so freely received. "Be kind to one another, tenderhearted, forgiving one another, as God in Christ has forgiven you. Therefore be imitators of God" (Eph 4:32—5:1; 2 Cor 5:16-21).

Receiving God's Forgiveness

It may be difficult for some of us to forgive because we have not really learned how to receive God's forgiveness for ourselves. Underneath our anger at others is a burden of unpardoned guilt and unrelieved shame. I continue to be amazed at the number of Christians I meet who believe they must somehow measure up before God will love them. They have heard it a million times, but they still have not received the sweet release of God's mercy. These words have fallen on closed ears, "By grace you have been saved through faith, and this is not your own doing; it is the gift of God—not the result of works, so that no one may boast" (Eph 2:8-9). Because they think God has a ledger system to balance their sins and good works, they keep an account of every wrong done to them as well.

The key to receiving God's forgiveness is to admit our need for it. We receive pardon by asking for it: "If we confess our sins, he who is faithful and just will forgive us our sins and cleanse us from all unrighteousness" (1 Jn 1:9). Often we confess our sins quietly in prayer, but some things we can only shake by confessing them to another Christian and hearing that person remind us of the good news of God's forgiveness for even *that* sin. I know someone who had been a prostitute before becoming a Christian. Though he acknowledged God's forgiveness and trusted that Christ died for him, he never really felt forgiven for all the shameful things he had done. That release finally came when he was able to confess his shame to a Christian counselor and a men's support group. Then he found the wisdom of James's advice, "Confess your sins to one another, and pray for one another, so that you may be healed" (Jas 5:16). No matter who we are or what we have done, there is grace to be found in the confession of sin to another member of the body of Christ.

When we truly appreciate that God forgives all our sins through Christ, then we understand that we have been given that same power to forgive others any wrong they do to us. Offering forgiveness to others is another secret to effective praying. When we come to God in prayer, we confess our sins and offer mercy to others. This is how we find forgiveness in prayer. "Forgive us our debts, as we also have forgiven our debtors."

Questions for Further Reflection

1. Are you aware of something you have done that you need God's forgiveness for?

2. Is there someone you find it difficult to forgive? Why?

3. Is there someone you prefer to avoid? Ponder that relationship. Does your avoidance signal unforgiveness on your part?

4. Why do you think some things and some people are harder to forgive than others?

5. How is confession of sin related to praying the first petition, that God's holy name be honored?

6. What have you noticed about bitter people?

10

Praying Through Trials & Temptations

And do not bring us to the time of trial,
but rescue us from the evil one.
MATTHEW 6:13

The greatest enemy of the Christian and the church is not the obvious evil but the apparent good. If the ship is only slightly off course for the entire journey, it still ends up far from its destination. The Crusades are one sad example. Christians prosecuted their holy wars with passion, thinking God was pleased. In retrospect their apparent good was an obvious evil. Temptation had prevailed, and neither the crusaders nor their victims were rescued from it. Far less extreme, but nevertheless destructive, are more common daily temptations to gossip, to distort tax returns, and to look longingly at someone with whom we are not married.

Jesus was tempted throughout his ministry to alter his course. He knew firsthand how distracting and disorienting spiritual attack and oppressive opponents could be. "In every respect," says the author of Hebrews, he "has been tested as we are, yet without sin" (Heb 4:15). In the oven of spiritual warfare, Jesus forged a prayer life that he wanted his disciples to arm themselves with too. If we are to honor God's name, seek God's kingdom, and walk in God's ways, we must be wise about the forces poised against God's people and learn to pierce them with prayer. So Jesus teaches us to pray through testing, trials, and temptations (all proper ways to translate the word rendered "time of trial," *peirasmos*, in this final petition of the Lord's Prayer).

To learn how Jesus faced temptations and trials, let us consider his behavior on two occasions. Just after his baptism, Jesus had his first face-to-face encounter with the devil. We should note that this temptation came *while* he fasted and prayed for forty days (Lk 4:2). It is a comfort and a warning that Jesus experienced what we do in prayer. It is ironic that we often face the greatest temptations and distractions just as we especially devote ourselves to prayer. Jesus' experience warns us to be wise as we pray. After forty days of fasting Jesus was physically weak and famished, making the first of three temptations that much more powerful. "The tempter came and said to him, 'If you are the Son of God, command these stones to become loaves of bread' " (Mt 4:3). With his stomach growling, Jesus rebukes the temptation with a reminder that God's word and God's will are of supreme importance for the faithful: "One does not live by bread alone, but by every word that comes from the mouth of God" (Mt 4:4, citing Deut 8:3). The devil then tempts Jesus to test God by throwing himself off the temple. Jesus rebukes this advance by citing Deuteronomy 6:16, "Do not put the Lord your God to the test" (Mt 4:7). Finally, the devil agrees to surrender the world to Jesus if Jesus surrenders himself to the devil. This is a temptation to fulfill Jesus' mission without the cross, but it requires Jesus to break God's will. So Jesus counters, "Away with you, Satan! for it is written, 'Worship the Lord your God, and serve only him' "

(Mt 4:10, citing Deut 6:13).

Jesus' method of dealing with each temptation underscores the importance of knowing and doing God's will by knowing the Scriptures. In the Lord's Prayer we have already prayed "your will be done," and I emphasized in chapter seven the interconnectedness between doing God's will and knowing and obeying God's Word. Jesus models this as he defends himself against the devil by announcing God's will as revealed in Scripture. When the devil tries his hand at Scripture twisting, Jesus untangles the mess with a clear response from the Scriptures. Jesus models in his encounter with the devil what he teaches us to pray in the Lord's Prayer.

A much later occasion also shows us how Jesus faced severe testing with prayer. On the night before his arrest and crucifixion, Jesus faced the greatest trial of his life (Mt 26:36-44 par. Mk 14:32-39 and Lk 22:40-46). Was he to submit to God's will and face a gruesome and humiliating execution, or would he opt out? He wrestles with God in Gethsemane, much as his ancestor Jacob had done many centuries before when God changed his name to Israel, meaning "wrestles with God" (Gen 32:24-30). Amid his spiritual struggle with God, Jesus reminds his disciples of his instructions about prayer, "Pray that you may not come into the time of trial; the spirit indeed is willing, but the flesh is weak" (Mt 26:41). Prayer is the source of Jesus' strength and resolve, and afterward he willingly submits to arrest and the cross. Prayer had refreshed him in his Father's will.

Jesus never gave in to temptation, but he knew its power over our human constitution. When the pressure is the greatest and our weaknesses are exposed, it is then that trials and temptations present themselves. And they are not simply neutral. Spiritual attack has a focus: to trip us up and undo our faithfulness to God. "Deliver us from the evil one" reminds us that there is an intelligent opposition lined up against us. Since most of us have learned the Lord's Prayer slightly differently, we should clarify this translation, "rescue us from the evil one."

The Evil One

The New Revised Standard Version rightly translates "the evil one" *(tou ponērou)*, though most of us have learned the King James Version's "deliver us from evil."[1] The Greek favors the NRSV, but we are left with three possible interpretations of "the evil one": the devil, the evil person or the evil thing. As we look at Matthew's Gospel, we see that Jesus uses "the evil one" in all three ways. If we pray the Lord's Prayer in the King James Version, "Deliver us from evil," we should keep all three of these in mind.

1. The devil. It is clear that Jesus does not see evil as some mysterious power set blindly against God, but as a directed force by the one opposing God's purposes: the devil—the tempter, Satan, Beelzebub. There is no other way to explain Jesus' encounter with the devil just after his baptism. We are given no particular description of the devil's appearance, as he often manifests himself through people and "even disguises himself as an angel of light" (2 Cor 11:14). It is obvious that Jesus believes in the reality of the devil, and he uses the phrase "the evil one" *(tou ponērou)* outside of the Lord's Prayer to say so (Mt 5:37; 13:38).

2. Hurtful people. Jesus also uses this expression, "the evil one," to describe human beings who are set against God's purposes. Just as the devil opposes the purposes of God, so do human beings; often they work in tandem (see especially Mt 16:23). In the previous chapter before the Lord's Prayer in Matthew, Jesus says not to resist "the evil one," turning the other cheek when struck (Mt 5:39). A few verses later, Jesus speaks of evil people who receive sunshine and rain in the same measure as the righteous (Mt 5:45). Following "rescue us from the evil one" in Matthew, Jesus returns our attention to people who have wronged us (Mt 6:14-15). There are many other examples of people opposing the purposes of God in Jesus' life and teaching who are labeled "evil ones" (Mt 12:35; 18:32; 22:10).

3. Stumbling blocks. A third possibility is also suggested by the context of the Lord's Prayer in Matthew. We are told ten verses after the Lord's Prayer that the "eye" can be an evil thing that trips us up (Mt 6:23), a point Jesus refers to both before and after the Lord's Prayer in the Sermon on the Mount. He had just said, "If your right eye causes you to sin, tear it out and throw it away; it is better for you to lose one of your members than for your whole body to be thrown into hell" (Mt 5:29). Likewise he reminds us not to overlook the "log" in our own eye as we scrutinize the speck in another's (Mt 7:1-5).[2] When we pray "deliver us from the evil thing," we concede that temptation sometimes originates within us. Too often we find, "I have met the enemy, and the enemy is me."

When we pray this final petition of the Lord's Prayer, then, we are encouraged to use it, like the other petitions, as an outline, a reminder to pray about the evil beings, people and things that we face as we seek to be faithful to God. If we want to lead lives that honor God's holy name, then we need God's help to weave our way through the "slings and arrows of outrageous fortune" that we face day by day. Like recovering addicts in twelve-step programs, all of us benefit from "improving our conscious daily contact with God," and the path to victorious living is paved with prayer. It is encouraging to learn elsewhere in Scripture that God has promised to always answer this prayer: "No testing has overtaken you that is not common to everyone. God is faithful, and he will not let you be tested beyond your strength, but with the testing he will also provide the way out so that you may be able to endure it" (1 Cor 10:13).

Spiritual Warfare

Westerners tend to be mechanistic in our worldview. Angels and demons do not belong in our Newtonian universe, and there are many Christians who doubt or deny the existence of a personal devil. Their thinking is that the devil is an antiquated way of explaining phenomena that we now understand better and have different words to describe. What the ancients called demonization, we call mental illness, and so forth.[3] In practice, Westerners sometimes update these parts of the Bible to fit their mechanistic worldview.

Those who doubt the devil's existence might be interested in reading C. S. Lewis's *The Screwtape Letters*. One of the devil's favorite temptations, muses Lewis, is to tempt us to disbelieve in his existence so he can go about his affairs unnoticed. Lewis chides, "There are two equal and opposite errors into which our race can fall about the devils. One is to disbelieve in their existence. The other is to believe, and to feel an excessive and unhealthy interest in them. They themselves are equally pleased by both errors, and hail a materialist and a magician with the same delight."[4] Allow me to suggest two cautions for any reader who might have a hard time praying "rescue us from the evil one" to include the devil.

First, Jesus taught this prayer, and he even prays this way for his disciples: "I am not asking you to take them out of the world, but I ask you to protect them from the evil one" (Jn 17:15). We call him Lord and revere his teaching, as we should. So we should respect his teaching regarding evil as being personally directed by the devil. Few of the requests in the Lord's Prayer fit our natural inclinations, but in each of them Jesus teaches us something essential about our walk with God and the practice of prayer. He devotes one-sixth of his compendium on prayer to the subject of spiritual warfare and the wiles of the devil. If Jesus is right, ignoring the devil's existence is foolish. Facts that we do not face squarely have a habit of stabbing us in the back!

Second, we should listen to our Christian brothers and sisters around the world who testify to the reality of spiritual warfare. Countless Christians witness to the importance of this sixth petition of the Lord's Prayer as they seek to know Christ and to make Christ known. Jesus taught us to pray "rescue us from the evil one." Those who obey him in this matter have found new spiritual power and solutions to problems that could not be solved in conventional ways.[5] Their experience explains the understanding of the earliest Christians that they needed to "put on the whole armor of God" in order to "stand against the wiles of the devil" (Eph 6:11).

> For our struggle is not against enemies of blood and flesh, but against the rulers, against the authorities, against the cosmic powers of this present darkness, against the spiritual forces of evil in the heavenly places. Therefore take up the whole armor of God, so that you may be able to withstand on that evil day, and having done everything, to stand firm. Stand therefore, and fasten the belt of truth around your waist, and put on the breastplate of righteousness. As shoes for your feet put on whatever will make you ready to proclaim the gospel of peace. With all of these, take the shield of faith, with which you will be able to quench all the flaming arrows of the evil one. Take the helmet of salvation, and the sword of the Spirit, which is the word of God. Pray in the Spirit at all times in every prayer and supplication. To that end keep alert and always persevere in supplication for all the saints. (Eph 6:12-18)

Then and now, Christians have found spiritual warfare to be part and parcel of a walk with God.

This is not to claim that there is a demon behind everything that goes wrong. Our increased understanding of mental illness has led to many treatments that relieve people's suffering. But there are many patients who do not respond to treatment, and their mental problems may well have a spiritual cause.[6] As C. Peter Wagner puts it, we shouldn't think that there is a demon behind every bush, but "demons are, in fact, behind some bushes."[7] If nothing else, it is wise to remain open to spiritual explanations of physical and psychological problems, as well as biological and mechanical explanations.

Temptation is a part of the Christian life. It comes from all quarters, within and without. We are tempted to remain bitter, to hate, to fear, to gossip, to lust, to be selfish, to be self-righteous, to give up—and the list goes on. Furthermore, we often face circumstances that test our mettle as believers. These trials subject our faith to a stress test and build character in us. We should face all trials, tests and temptations prayerfully, seeking deliverance from the circumstances and opponents we face.

Conclusion

With this final petition of the Lord's Prayer we have prayed for all of life, from God in heaven to the devil in hell. All of life is to be faced with prayer. We have spent these seven chapters exploring the Lord's Prayer. In the next chapter we will turn our attention to a question that perplexes wannabe believers in a scientific age: does God really perform miracles and healing, circumventing the system of natural cause and effect?

Questions for Further Reflection

1. Reflect on a time in your life when you went through a period of testing.

    a. What challenges did you face?

    b. How were you victorious?

    c. What failures did you experience?

    d. What was the most difficult aspect of your testing?

    e. What helped you get through it?

2. Do you believe in spiritual warfare? Why or why not? How do you make sense of Jesus' encounters with the evil one?

3. Where are you facing temptation in your life right now?

4. What are the three possible meanings of "the evil one"?

11

Praying for Healing & Miracles

Very truly, I tell you, the one who believes
in me will also do the works that I do
and, in fact, will do greater works than these,
because I am going to the Father.
JOHN 14:12

There once was a funeral for a circus master in England. The funeral procession was like a parade as circus performers and animals from all over the country paid tribute. Behind the hearse trailed circus acts of all sorts: jugglers, trained lions, stunt ponies, trapeze artists and many more. At the end of the column were six trained elephants, each one conditioned to come into the performing circle and to sit on its own color stool—red, green, blue and so forth.

Out for a drive on that same day was a man in his new blue Jaguar. He came to a roundabout and had to wait for the last half of the funeral column to circle around in front of him and then out of the roundabout toward the mortuary. As the elephants circled past, the one used to sitting on the blue stool got confused. The roundabout reminded her of the circus ring, and so she rambled over and sat down on the front of the blue Jaguar, thinking she had found her place. Her weight crushed the fenders of the car down around the front wheels, disabling it.

The elephant's handler came running over, apologized profusely to the driver, exchanged insurance information, and then said, "I'm sorry but we've got to go." Off went the end of the funeral procession, and the roundabout was clear. The man in the Jaguar sat stunned in his crushed car. But even as he sat there, the nightmare grew worse. Along came a police officer who knocked on his window and asked him to move along. Rolling down his window, the driver said, "You'll never believe what just happened to me. An elephant came over, sat on the front of my car and crushed the fenders so I can't drive." Incredulous, the bobby began sniffing the air for the smell of alcohol and asked the driver to get out of the car. Eventually everything got worked out.

The moral of the story goes like this: just because you haven't seen it doesn't mean it didn't happen. This applies to divine healing too. Just because we haven't seen it doesn't mean it doesn't happen. The Gospels are united on this testimony: Jesus went about healing and working wonders as he taught and preached. Everywhere Jesus went, the sick and infirm were brought to him for his healing touch. Epileptics, lepers, the lame and deaf and blind. Each time he healed, Jesus demonstrated his divine nature and the presence of the kingdom.

Jesus bestowed this same healing power on his disciples. To pray for healing is another way of praying for the coming of the kingdom. While he was still with them, he sent them out in pairs with the instructions, "cure the sick who are there, and say to them, 'The kingdom of God has come near to you' " (Lk 10:9). After his crucifixion and resurrection, the healing works continued and confirmed the presence of the kingdom and the validity of the church as God's chosen vehicle. Jesus' words were fulfilled: "Very truly, I tell you, the one who believes in me will also do the works that I do and, in fact, will do greater works than these, because I am going to the Father" (Jn 14:12). Praying for healing is praying Jesus' way.

Some Christians believe that miraculous powers ended with the death of the first apostles, but most believe in praying for healing. There is a widespread belief inside and outside the church that prayer can help people recover from injury, illness and disease. According to a recent survey, 79 percent of Americans believe so, and 56 percent claim their faith has aided their recovery from sickness or injury.[1] Hospitalization mobilizes the prayer chains: "Heal John's heart." "Use the surgeons to heal the blockage in Mary's stomach." "Heal our pastor's flu so he can preach on Sunday." "Heal the pain in Ruth's back and the tumor in Bill's brain."

Technique does not seem to matter greatly. Sometimes we lay on hands for healing as Jesus did. "Are any among you sick? They should call for the elders of the church and have them pray over them, anointing them with oil in the name of the Lord. The prayer of faith will save [heal] the sick, and the Lord will raise them up" (Jas 5:14-15). Other times we simply pray from where we are, and the healing power goes out (see Mk 5:25-34). Once Jesus used his saliva to make a mud balm, spreading it on a blind man's eyes and "saying to him, 'Go, wash in the pool of Siloam.' . . . Then he went and washed and came back able to see" (Jn 9:6-7). The presence of the kingdom is demonstrated as God hears people's cries and responds to them with a healing touch.

When Prayer Does Not Work

Jesus did not heal everybody. There were crowds that he walked past, and there were people he did not deliver. There is no evidence that Jesus' prayers for healing ever failed, but the disciples experienced the frustration of unanswered prayer. Once they prayed for a boy who was unable to speak and had seizures. The father of that boy bluntly said to Jesus, "I asked your disciples to cast it out, but they could not do so" (Mk 9:18). Frankly, I find great encouragement in knowing that the disciples, like me, experienced the frustration of unanswered prayer.

There are various explanations for why some prayers go unanswered: unconfessed sin, undetected doubt, unyielded pray-er, and so on. But all we really know is that some of our prayers are not answered as we ask them. We pray for healing, but the cancer runs its course and kills its victim. We may rationalize that the deceased actually was healed, that is, received the ultimate healing transformation that comes with entering eternal life. This is true, but it does not change the fact that we did not receive the healing that we prayed for.

Jesus has already prepared us for unanswered prayer with his experience in the garden of Gethsemane where he prayed, "Let this cup pass from me." He was yielded to God's purpose even as he asked this, so he continued, "yet not what I want but what you want" (Mt 26:39). Again the Lord's Prayer serves as our guide to prayer. We pray "your will be done," submitting our desires to God's purposes. We ask sincerely, but then we yield ourselves to the wisdom and mercy of God, confident "that all things work together for good for those who love God, who are called according to his purpose" (Rom 8:28).

Those who suffer from chronic or acute pain can take some cues from how Jesus prayed through his pain as he faced the agony of the cross in the garden of Gethsemane. He prayed to avoid temptation, he involved others in praying with him, and he yielded himself up with "not my will but yours be done" (Lk 22:40-46 par. Mt 26:36-44 and Mk 14:32-39). These four aspects of Jesus' prayer form an acronym that reminds us how to pray through pain (P.A.I.N.):

Pray.

Avoid temptation.

Involve others.

Not my will but God's be done.

Acute or chronic pain challenges our faith more than anything. We are tempted to cry out, "Why?" and "Where are you, God?" God always reveals himself eventually, but the peace that accompanies prayer can bring great comfort and relief to us in our painful struggle.

Persistence in Prayer

When pain persists and pressures mount, we may tend to stop praying. We may interpret long-term outcomes in terms of temporary circumstances with a gloomy, "What difference will praying make anyway?" Jesus anticipated such discouragement, and so he "told them a parable about their need to pray always and not to lose heart" (Lk 18:1). The hero of this story is the persistent widow who kept pounding and pounding on the judge's door until he granted her justice because of her tenacity. Jesus concludes,

> Listen to what the unjust judge says. And will not God grant justice to his chosen ones who cry to him day and night? Will he delay long in helping them? I tell you, he will quickly grant justice to them. And yet, when the Son of Man comes, will he find faith on earth? (Lk 18:6-8)

The widow had no great technique. She simply persisted. The judge calls her a bother (Lk 18:5). Jesus tells the story to encourage all of us not to give up when we pray. He values tenacity over technique, and wants us to remain persistent in prayer. Indeed, the technique he teaches is to keep bothering God with our prayers!

Prayer for healing is anticipated in the Lord's Prayer. As we pray for the wholeness in a person's body, mind or spirit, we are praying for the coming of the kingdom. When prayers seem to go unanswered, we yield ourselves in trust, "Your will be done." All the while we continue to pray for any and every circumstance, not losing heart, not giving up. The One who teaches us to pray is the One who has promised to hear and heed our prayers.

Questions for Further Reflection

1. Have you or someone you know ever witnessed a miraculous answer to prayer? Reflect on what happened.

2. Do you expect God to answer prayers that seek miraculous results? Why or why not?

3. Do you know someone who needs healing right now? Pause and pray for that person.

4. What discourages you from praying? How can you break through this barrier?

5. What is the longest you have prayed for something? What was the outcome? Why do you think it took so long to receive an answer?

12

Jesus Understands the Struggle of Prayer

For we do not have a high priest who is unable to sympathize
with our weaknesses, but we have one who in
every respect has been tested as we are, yet without sin. Let
us therefore approach the throne of grace with boldness,
so that we may receive mercy and find
grace to help in time of need.
HEBREWS 4:15-16

Many *Christian pray-ers experience guilt and frustration. This*
is due in large part to false expectations that we have
created in regard to how much we should pray and
how much we should expect when we pray. But Jesus teaches that
prayer is a gift, not a burden. He counsels us to pray simply, from
the heart, with few words. He reminds us to always be yielded to
God's will and God's ways. What we ask for in prayer may not
always be the answer a loving God knows we need.

On the other extreme are those who boast about their spirituality. Perhaps they see many answers to their prayers. For them,
the gift of prayer can become a badge of spiritual pride and
superiority. Jesus understands this struggle too and cautions
against self-righteousness in prayer, devoting a whole parable to
the subject (Lk 18:9-14): "He also told this parable to some who
trusted in themselves that they were righteous and regarded
others with contempt" (Lk 18:9). Perhaps inside all of us lurks a

Pharisee who feels superior to others. Turning the tables, Jesus says that God is pleased instead with the sinner who is contrite and humble, who prays, "God be merciful to me, a sinner!" The Pharisee's fate is predictable because "all who exalt themselves will be humbled." Whether we are tempted to pride or to guilt about our prayer life, the reminder is the same. Prayer is the gift of a relationship with God.

Jesus understands how we struggle with the gift of prayer, and it is great news to know that "he always lives to make intercession" for us (Heb 7:25). But even more than that, he offers us needed help in prayer through the gift of the Holy Spirit. The Holy Spirit, God's presence in our lives, is the greatest daily aid we have for prayer. Understanding Jesus' teaching on prayer and embracing the ever present Advocate and Guide, the Holy Spirit (Jn 14:13-16; Lk 11:13), we have great encouragement and assistance to enjoy the gift of prayer we have been given.

Because Jesus understands the struggle of prayer, he told a parable "about their need to pray always and not lose heart" (Lk 18:1). We need that same encouragement, and we find it throughout the teaching of Jesus. Whether we pray formally or informally, whether we use the words of the ancient people of God or spontaneously lift our own praise and prayer, Jesus encourages us to come boldly to God seeking the gift and goodness of a renewed relationship. Whenever and however we pray, "let us therefore approach the throne of grace with boldness, so that we may receive mercy and find grace to help in time of need" (Heb 4:16).

Appendix

Suggestions for Praying the Lord's Prayer Alone & in Groups

Praying Alone

Once you understand the six basic petitions of the Lord's Prayer, it is easy to create a prayer guide in your mind or on a sheet of paper that reminds you of the kinds of things you can pray about. Recite aloud each petition in the Lord's Prayer, and then pause to reflect and pray spontaneously about each area, focusing on the parts that seem most appropriate for the day. At the end, pray through the Lord's Prayer—slowly, word for word—as you remember and affirm the time you have just spent in prayer. Racing through the Lord's Prayer is a sure way for its words to become "vain repetition."

Praying in Groups

Assign one person to lead the prayer. That person guides the prayer time by inviting all participants to pray spontaneously about each area that the Lord's Prayer suggests. Encourage them to spark off of one another's prayers, as this is a good way to learn more and more about praying the Lord's Prayer. The leader begins, "Our Father who art in heaven, hallowed be thy name," and then pauses. Several minutes are allowed for participants who would like to pray aloud about this. When a silence settles in, the leader continues, "Thy kingdom come," and so forth. When the group has prayed through the entire prayer as an outline, encourage everyone to join together as the Lord's Prayer is prayed in unison—slowly—at the end of the prayer time. If the group includes ten participants, this approach will easily fill an hour.

Praying in Public Worship

As a variation of the group version of this prayer, the leader can recite each line slowly, allowing a minute or two of silence for the congregation to silently pray about each part of the Lord's Prayer. At the end, invite everyone to join together in slowly praying the Lord's Prayer in unison. Alternatively, the congregation could break into groups of three or four and pray in their small groups as the leader guides them through the prayer, joining together to pray the Lord's Prayer in unison when the time of guided prayer is completed.

Some churches emphasize the family nature of this prayer since it begins, "*Our* Father . . ." The prayer takes on a much more corporate feel if people join hands with those near them before praying this prayer. The physical act of joining hands emphasizes the communal nature of praying together with and for one another.

Notes

Chapter 1: Introduction

[1] Oscar Cullmann, *Prayer in the New Testament*, trans. J. Bowden (Minneapolis: Fortress, 1995), p. xiii.

[2] A complementary approach is the daily devotional by Eugene H. Peterson, *Praying with Jesus: A Year of Daily Prayers and Reflections on the Words and Actions of Jesus* (San Francisco: HarperSanFrancisco, 1993).

[3] Thomas Merton, *The Sign of Jonas* (New York: Harcourt, Brace and Company, 1953), p. 198.

Chapter 2: How Jesus Prayed

[1] See *The Works of John Wesley*, 3rd ed. (Peabody, Mass.: Hendrickson, 1991), 8:270-71.

[2] Robin Norwood, *Women Who Love Too Much* (New York: Pocket Books, 1985).

[3] It should not concern us that John's Gospel does not record this feature of Jesus' prayer life. In fact, he does not even use the Greek words that we ordinarily translate "prayer." He simply identifies prayer as "asking." His Gospel and his focus are distinct from the other three in many ways, and this is largely due to his evangelistic motivation in writing his Gospel: "But these are written so that you may come to believe that Jesus is the Messiah, the Son of God, and that through believing you may have life in his name" (Jn 20:31). He has selected his presentation of Jesus because of this motive and has intentionally left out much that could have been said (20:30; 21:25).

[4] I use the abbreviation *par.* (for "parallel") to show that the passages quoted are the same or similar in the other Gospel accounts.

Chapter 3: Jesus & Jewish Prayer

[1] Oscar Cullmann, *Prayer in the New Testament*, trans. J. Bowden (Minneapolis:

Fortress, 1995), p. xiv.

[2]There are places where Jesus uses the word *Father* in a way that emphasizes his unique equality with God (Jn 5:18), but this is different from Jesus' instructions to us in our relating to God as adopted children (Mt 6:9).

[3]Joachim Jeremias, "The Lord's Prayer in Light of Recent Research," in *The Prayers of Jesus*, trans. John Reumann (Philadelphia: Fortress, 1967), pp. 82-107.

[4]See Patrick D. Miller, *They Cried to the Lord: The Form and Theology of Biblical Prayer* (Minneapolis: Fortress, 1994), pp. 329-30; James H. Charlesworth, "A Caveat on Textual Transmission and the Meaning of *Abba*: A Study of the Lord's Prayer," in *The Lord's Prayer and Other Prayer Texts from the Greco-Roman Era*, ed. J. Charlesworth, M. Harding and M. Kiley (Valley Forge, Penn.: Trinity Press International, 1994), pp. 1-14.

[5]The same word for "sing a hymn" *(hymnesantes)* is used, for example, in the Greek version of Ps 21:23; 64:14; 70:8.

[6]Gordon J. Bahr, "The Use of the Lord's Prayer in the Primitive Church," *Journal of Biblical Literature* 84 (1965): 153-59.

[7]Jakob J. Petuchowski and Michael Brocke, eds., *The Lord's Prayer and Jewish Liturgy* (New York: Seabury, 1978); Brad Young, *The Jewish Background to the Lord's Prayer* (Austin: Center for Judaic-Christian Studies, 1984); J. Charlesworth, M. Harding and M. Kiley, eds., *The Lord's Prayer and Other Prayer Texts from the Greco-Roman Era* (Valley Forge, Penn.: Trinity Press International, 1994).

Chapter 4: Praying the Lord's Prayer

[1]See James H. Charlesworth, "A Caveat on Textual Transmission and the Meaning of *Abba*: A Study of the Lord's Prayer," in *The Lord's Prayer and Other Prayer Texts from the Greco-Roman Era*, ed. J. Charlesworth, M. Harding and M. Kiley (Valley Forge, Penn.: Trinity Press International, 1994), pp. 1-14.

[2]Tertullian *De Oratione* 1, as cited and translated by Gordon J. Bahr, "The Use of the Lord's Prayer in the Primitive Church," *Journal of Biblical Literature* 84 (1965): 154.

[3]Origen *Peri Euchēs* 18.1, as cited and translated by Bahr, "Use of the Lord's Prayer," pp. 153-54.

[4]See, for example, Bill Hybels, *Too Busy Not to Pray: Slowing Down to Be with God* (Downers Grove, Ill.: InterVarsity Press, 1988), pp. 51-60.

Chapter 5: Seeking God's Face in Prayer

[1]See, for example, Dieter Zeller, "God as Father in the Proclamation and in the Prayer of Jesus," in *Standing Before God: Studies on Prayer in Scriptures and in Tradition with Essays in Honor of John M. Oesterreicher,* ed. Asher Finkel and

Lawrence Frizzell (New York: KTAV, 1981), pp. 117-29.

[2]Oscar Cullmann, *Prayer in the New Testament,* trans. J. Bowden (Minneapolis: Fortress, 1995), p. 4.

[3]Contemporary English Version (New York: American Bible Society, 1995).

[4]Joachim Jeremias, "Abba," in *The Prayers of Jesus,* trans. John Bowden (Philadelphia: Fortress, 1967), pp. 11-65.

[5]James Barr, "Abba Isn't 'Daddy,' " *Journal of Theological Studies* 39 (1988): 28-47.

[6]See also Joseph A. Fitzmyer, "*Abba* and Jesus' Relation to God," in *Études sur les Synoptiques et les Actes* (Paris: Cerf, 1985), pp. 15-38; James H. Charlesworth, "A Caveat on Textual Transmission and the Meaning of *Abba:* A Study of the Lord's Prayer," in *The Lord's Prayer and Other Prayer Texts from the Greco-Roman Era,* ed. J. Charlesworth, M. Harding and M. Kiley (Valley Forge, Penn.: Trinity Press International, 1994), pp. 1-14. "Wrong as it is, it deserves mention not only because of its extensive dissemination beyond the walls of academia but also because its influence can be detected even in the work of respected scholars" (John Ashton, "Abba," in *Anchor Bible Dictionary* [New York: Doubleday, 1992], 1:7). For example, the error is repeated in an otherwise careful and thoughtful book, John Killinger's *Rediscovering New Testament Prayer: Boldness and Blessing in the Name of Jesus* (San Francisco: Harper & Row, 1992).

[7]Brennan Manning, *Abba's Child: The Cry of the Heart for Intimate Belonging* (Colorado Springs, Colo.: NavPress, 1994), p. 18.

[8]For example, P. R. Smith, *Is It Okay to Call God "Mother"?* (Peabody, Mass.: Hendrickson, 1993).

Chapter 6: Seeking God's Rule in Prayer

[1]Throughout this book I rely on Dale Bruner's lectures on Matthew. His teaching helped me make the Lord's Prayer an essential part of my prayer life. See Frederick Dale Bruner, *Matthew: A Commentary,* vols. 1-2 (Dallas: Word, 1990).

[2]Raymond E. Brown believes the entire Lord's Prayer is laced with end-time innuendoes. See his "The Pater Noster as an Eschatological Prayer," in *New Testament Essays* (London: Geoffrey Chapman, 1965), pp. 217-53.

Chapter 7: Seeking God's Will in Prayer

[1]Oscar Cullmann, *Prayer in the New Testament,* trans. J. Bowden (Minneapolis: Fortress, 1995), p. 10.

[2]Charles H. Spurgeon, "David's Prayer in the Cave," in *Twelve Sermons on Prayer* (Grand Rapids, Mich.: Baker Book House, 1990), p. 149.

[3]Ibid.

[4]C. Peter Wagner, *Churches That Pray* (Ventura, Calif.: Regal, 1993), p. 48.

[5]*The Methodist Service Book* (London: Methodist Publishing House, 1975), p. D10.

[6]Leslie Weatherhead's study of the will of God is the classic on the subject, and Rebecca Laird has adapted it for a thorough exploration of the subject by individual readers or study groups in her *The Will of God: A Workbook* (Nashville: Abingdon, 1995).

Chapter 8: Seeking God's Hand in Prayer

[1]So, for example, Jean Carmignac, *Recherches sur le "Notre Père"* (Paris: Éditions Letouzey & Ané, 1969), p. 221.

[2]Bruce M. Metzger, "How Many Times Does *Epiousios* Occur Outside the Lord's Prayer?" *The Expository Times* 69 (1957-58): 52-54.

[3]Ibid., p. 52. Whereas Metzger only knew of this one confirmed occurrence of *epiousios* outside of the Lord's Prayer in the late 1950s, a computer search of Greek papyri now reveals at least three usages of the term (five others are reconstructed possibilities for the texts). Most important is *Oxyrhynchus Papyrus* PMert 18.22, which can be dated to about A.D. 161. It mentions a trip to Alexandria to obtain *epiousan* and "other things pertaining to everyday life" *(heteron biotikon).*

[4]C. Peter Wagner, *Churches That Pray* (Ventura, Calif.: Regal, 1993), p. 42.

[5]Thomas T. Poleman, "Obstacles to Famine Relief," in *Grolier's Academic American Encyclopedia,* on-line ed. (Grolier Electronic Publishers, 1994).

Chapter 9: Finding Forgiveness in Prayer

[1]We could render it "seventy times seven," or 490. Both numbers vastly exceed Peter's expectations. The point is to keep on forgiving without limit.

[2]The best book I have seen on the difficulty of forgiving others is Lewis B. Smedes, *Forgive and Forget: Healing the Hurts We Don't Deserve* (San Francisco: Harper & Row, 1984).

Chapter 10: Praying Through Trials & Temptations

[1]"Evil" would be the appropriate translation if the article *the (ho)* had not been used, as in Matthew 7:11, 17; 12:34, 39; 13:49; 16:4.

[2]And see Matthew 20:15.

[3]One example along the lines of "demythologizing" the language of the Bible is Walter Wink, *Naming the Powers: The Language of Power in the New Testament,* vol. 1, *The Powers* (Philadelphia: Fortress, 1984).

[4]C. S. Lewis, *The Screwtape Letters* (New York· Macmillan, 1962), p. 3.

[5]Those of us new to this sphere would do well to read some recent books by C. Peter Wagner, including *Warfare Prayer: How to Seek God's Power and Protection in the Battle to Build His Kingdom* (Ventura, Calif.: Regal, 1992) and *Prayer Shield:*

How to Intercede for Pastors, Christian Leaders and Others on the Spiritual Frontlines (Ventura, Calif.: Regal, 1992). We need not agree with all that Wagner writes to appreciate the point of view that he shares with Jesus: there is a devil at work in the world who seeks to subvert God's people and God's purposes.

[6]See M. Scott Peck, *People of the Lie: The Hope for Healing Human Evil* (New York: Simon & Schuster, 1983).

[7]Wagner, *Warfare Prayer,* p. 85.

Chapter 11: Praying for Healing & Miracles

[1]Tony McNichol, "The New Faith in Medicine: Believing in God May Be Good for Your Health," *USA Weekend,* April 5-7, 1996, p. 5.